SPEAK WITH PASSION SPEAK WITH POWER!

Transform Inexperience and the Fear of Public Speaking into Energy, Know-How and Results!

Pamela Gilbreath Kelly, M.A.

First printing: April 2007

Upward and Onward Publishing

www.upwardandonwardpublishing.com

P.O. Box 21681

Long Beach, California 90801

Book Design by www.KareenRoss.com

Cartoons by Ray Harris www.rayharrisstudio.com

Library of Congress Cataloging-in-Publication Data is available from the Library of Congress

ISBN 978-0-9791001-0-9

First Edition 2007

Dedication

To my father, 2nd Lt. Ray "Buck" Gilbreath,

United States Air Force, World War II;

September 1, 1923 – March 6, 1944.

And to my mother and step-father,

Mary Florence Sharp and Roger Sharp.

Thank you for giving me the world.

What People Are Saying

"Even if you don't do any public speaking, the way you present yourself to others says a lot about your confidence and self-esteem. This book will help you own your power and present yourself authentically, as someone with self-worth."
—Janet Ault, Past President of PDQ Careers and of Women in Business;
Advisor, Dean's Advisory Council, College of Education, Purdue University

"This book is off-the-charts indispensable for those who truly want to further their public speaking skills! Pam puts together the tools to help you dig deep and explore yourself from the inside out to determine what obstacles hinder you in your speaking and how to overcome them."
—Beti Tsai Bergman, Attorney and Counselor at Law,
Law Offices of Beti Tsai Bergman, Los Angeles

"It's like having your own private tutor at your side! More than "must read," it is a MUST USE book for all of us."
—Jo Condrill, M.S., Speaker, Author, Consultant,
President, GoalMinds, Inc., http://www.goalminds.com

"I speak in public a lot and Pam helped me have more confidence and be more effective every time. This book captures the spirit of her coaching and will do the same for you."
—Antonio Cue, Co-owner and President, Chivas USA, Professional Soccer and Sports Club

"A must-read book that helps us transform our psychological and emotional fears into powerful, spoken words that inspire others."
—Henry Gellis, President, Center of the Cyclone, Inc. and Film Producer, Los Angeles

"With remarkable candor, Pam Kelly reflects on her own upbringing and insecurities to illustrate the psychological underpinnings of public speaking fears. Weaving inspirational case studies and focused exercises, she empowers her students to stand and deliver. Kelly's mantra for confident, congruent communication is deceptively simple: Be yourself, but on purpose."
—Matthew King, Former Vice President of Content, The Hollywood Reporter, Los Angeles

"You have always delivered powerful results and your book will benefit many. Your in-house seminars improved the presentation skills of many civil service employees, who are continuously asked to speak to community groups. Ultimately, it is the citizens of Los Angeles who benefit from your efforts."
—Abraham Navarro, General Superintendent, Executive Division,
Bureau of Street Services, Public Works, The City of Los Angeles

"People interested in improving their speaking skills will profit greatly, no matter what their starting point or frame of reference. As the book leads readers through a logical process of assessing, thinking, and planning, they emerge with the skills and confidence to speak with what else? Passion and Power!"
—George Nickle, Senior Management Specialist,
Metropolitan Water District of Southern California, Los Angeles

"I first worked with Pam when I was in my first management job out of college. With her guidance, I learned to speak with confidence, make myself heard and sell my message. Over the years, I've asked Pam to provide trainings at a number of different companies. Each time, I saw the transformation of people who truly wanted to improve themselves and their position by becoming powerful public speakers. With all the noise in the market, you need to be heard. Putting this book to use is one way to make it happen."
—Rich Ratkelis, Small Business Owner, Aliso Viejo, CA

"Beginning with the premise that we can overcome this common phobia, *Speak with Passion, Speak with Power!* shows us how to unleash our greatest potential as a public speaker by overcoming our fears and drawing upon a "bigger-than-life" purpose."
—Salle Redfield, Executive Producer, The Celestine Prophecy Movie

"Pamela Kelly's course is the most valuable thing I have done for my career. It not only exceeded my goal of becoming a more confident public speaker, but also taught me about successfully overcoming communication challenges faced in the everyday business world."
—Tyler Resh, Principal, 3 C Financial Partners LLC,
Manhattan Beach, CA

"Until I worked with Pam Kelly, I couldn't utter a word in front of an audience. Now I'm a successful speaker and workshop leader."
—Robin Fisher Roffer, President, Big Fish Branding and Fishnet, Los Angeles,
and Little Pond Productions, Atlanta

"*Speak with Passion, Speak with Power!* reflects Pam's 'heart-to-heart' approach to public speaking. As a native Japanese speaker who has been an officer in several professional organizations in Los Angeles over the years, this approach has worked very well for me and is the reason Pam has been my speech coach for over 15 years!"
—Hiroko Tatebe, Founder and Executive Director, GOLD, The Global Organization for Leadership and Diversity, Los Angeles, and Director of GEWEL, Global Enhancement of Women's Executive Leadership, Japan; Outstanding Business Woman of the Year,
Los Angeles Chapter of Women in Business

"This is an expertly instructive book with an invaluable process that helped transform me from a panic-stricken public-speaking neophyte into a self-assured speaker. As unbelievable as it sounds, I learned to actually _enjoy_ being in the spotlight. This book is a must for anyone who feels limited in their career by not being able to express themselves with confidence, authenticity and passion."
—Colin Ullyott, President, C & C Land Company, Canada

"I loved this book! I have learned so much from Pamela in my work both as a broadcaster and as a media coach, and now I am overjoyed to have her book as another rich source of her generosity, meticulous professionalism and wisdom."
—Leah Zinder, News Anchorwoman, IBA News, Israel Television's Channel One,
Jerusalem, Israel

Table of Contents

Part One: Take Charge of Your Fear

Chapter 1: Dismantle Your Fear

Chapter 2: Vanquish Inner Losers and Claim Your Fame

Chapter 3: Reprogram Your Fear

Chapter 4: Discover Your Big Purpose

Part Two: Take Simple Steps Consistently

Chapter 5: Ask the Right Questions

Chapter 6: Make a Plan

Chapter 7: Build a Container for Your Ideas

Chapter 8: Enrich Your Container

Chapter 9: Pour in the Juice!

Part Three: Go the Extra Mile

Chapter 10: Practice With Visuals

Chapter 11: Prepare for Questions and Answers

Chapter 12: Moving from Good to Great!

Acknowledgments

I am forever grateful to Dr. Patricia Hunt for hiring me to teach "Public Speaking for Professionals" at UCLA Extension over 20 years ago and who never said "No" to any of my course ideas. I appreciate the thousands of students and clients who have participated in my academic courses, corporate trainings and private coaching, in the United States, Hong Kong, Japan, Singapore and Thailand. They made it possible for me to write this book. In particular, I am grateful to Belinda Liok Tay, whose friendship and generosity made my teaching in Asia first possible.

I also want to single out the former students who became clients and friends and whose stories bring this book to life. First and foremost is Anne Reeves, who read each chapter as I wrote it and told me to make it clearer here and briefer there. Her friendship and support are priceless to me. I am indebted to Dorothy Breininger, whose courage and leadership inspire me to go for it! To Michael Almaraz, Katrina Aquiling-Dahl, Cliff Atkinson, Antoinette Byron, Karim Jaude, Dr. Roy Meals and Mamoru Shimokochi, thank you for your time, your genius and your generous hearts. And thank you for your memorable speeches, Bernard Caliman, Lisa Colicchio and Christine Kurimoto.

I want to take advantage of this opportunity to thank the folks at UCLA Extension Department of Business, Management and Legal Programs, for supporting me and my courses over the years—Renita Baily, Eddie Fisher and Department Director, Karim Cherif, and Program Director, Madge Claybion; Joyce Manson and Genevieve Lee, from the Dean's Office; and a special acknowledgment to my outstanding Program Reps, Martha Hochstrasser, Cathleen Dominquez and Zalina Walton.

I am blessed with my editor, Pat Brady; cartoonist, Ray Harris ("Raycasso") and book designer, Kareen Ross. They have been endlessly patient and perfect dance partners, effortlessly guiding and yielding as needed, and a joy to work with on this project.

I am honored to acknowledge my friend, Dr. Donald Dossey, whose bigger-than-life passion, power and generosity are a glorious gift to me. Thank you for your sense of humor, mentoring and encouragement over the years, Donald! And Henri Blits, thank you for your zany brilliance, enthusiastic support and many contributions to my classes.

Because this book is the culmination of many years of teaching for me, I want to express my indebtedness to my high school English and drama teachers, Eleanor Davis and George Scarborough, and to Roberta Winter, my speech teacher and theater director at Agnes Scott College, where I attended for two years. Thank you for seeing my possibilities, cheering me on and ultimately influencing me to become a teacher.

And finally there are those closest to me who give me so much space to be myself and to pursue my dreams. To my husband, Rick, who has the passion of his Italian mother, the patience of a saint and an outrageous sense of humor; our son, Eric, a testament to Shakespeare's words, "To thine own self be true;" and to our pets, Sweetie, Brownie, Robbie and Vixen: Thank you all for making sure I had plenty of endorphins to fuel this project. I couldn't have done it without you!

Introduction

"This little light of mine,
I'm gonna let it shine;
let it shine, let it shine, let it shine!"
— Old Negro Spiritual

Imagine yourself bringing all the passion and power that's in your soul to your speaking—and getting the results you want! Whether you're giving a presentation, teaching or interviewing for a job, it's not only possible but, by following these simple steps, it's probable!

Thousands of professionals, from Los Angeles and Boston to Singapore and Japan, and from every field imaginable—advertising and financial, marketing and medical, scientific and technical, and everything in between—have demonstrated that my system works. It's energizing, enjoyable and as you walk through it, my approach allows you to express more and more of the passion and power that's inside you.

After working with me, many of my students and clients have gone on to accomplish greater success—receiving promotions and raises, establishing and running their own companies, leading professional organizations, developing workshops and seminars, promoting their books and services through radio and television interviews, becoming professional speakers and winning speaking competitions.

So what is my system all about? Simply, it's about doing what works—preparing yourself for success and being yourself, on purpose. Luis Pasteur, the French scientist who developed the rabies vaccine, said, "Chance favors the prepared mind." He knew what he was talking about.

When Pasteur was developing his rabies vaccination, a little boy from his neighborhood was bitten by a rabid dog. The boy's parents knew about the famous scientist's experiments and begged him to use his untested vaccine on their child. Pasteur was hesitant, unsure if his drug would work. The parents pleaded with him and eventually Pasteur acquiesced. Fortunately, the vaccine did work and saved the little boy's life. Later, Pasteur would observe that "Chance favors the prepared mind."

Just as Pasteur had prepared himself to respond effectively and save the little boy, you can prepare yourself to be an effective speaker. Then, when your opportunity arrives, you're ready for it!

How to Use This Book

The principles of extraordinary communication apply to all speaking—whether in presentations, the classroom or in interviews. My primary focus, however, is on presentation skills for beginning speakers in any industry—the business professionals, technical folks and working moms who are ready to master public speaking and presentation skills. Throughout, I use the symbol of the ladder to represent the steps that will take you to your goals.

In Part One, "Take Charge of your Fear", I address the actions you can take to get control over the fear of public speaking. If fear is not at issue for you, then you may want to skip Part One and jump immediately into Part Two, "Take Simple Steps Consistently."

In Part One, I offer several approaches to mastering the fear of public speaking, from dismantling to reprogramming it. All of the approaches have exercises. Some of them suggest that you close your eyes as I lead you through relaxation and observation processes. Other exercises are more psychological in nature and involve your answering questions and writing or speaking your answers. You can write directly in this workbook. It isn't necessary to tackle all the approaches and do all the exercises straight through. I recommend you read through the approaches and choose to work with the ones you connect to. Then do only those exercises and move on to Part Two. Revisit Part One, however, from time to time, to experiment with the other approaches and complete more exercises, until fear is no longer an issue for you.

In Part Two, "Take Simple Steps Consistently", I will be walking you through the steps of preparing, rehearsing and delivering passionate, powerful and persuasive speaking—from the podium, in the classroom and at the interview. As you move through these chapters, you will be in action—doing some writing and a lot of speaking as you develop several presentations and apply the techniques that make you and your speaking extraordinary. The steps and techniques are like rungs on a ladder that take you to a higher level of mastery in your presentation.

In Part Three, "Go the Extra Mile", you will be practicing with visuals, preparing for questions, handling last minute details and moving from good to great! At this point, you and your speaking are one. You leap off the ladder and sail, carried by the force of your own passion and power.

A Summary of What You Will Need

Part One: Pen or pencil
        (Optional) Extra paper or journal, tape recorder

Part Two: Pen or pencil, note cards, wall mirror
        (Optional) Extra paper, tape recorder

Part Three: Pen or pencil, note cards
        (Optional) Extra paper, tape recorder

Ready? Before we take the plunge, I would like to welcome you and share a little about me and my journey.

Welcome!

My Story

There are two significant threads to my story. The first is that of a war orphan named Pamela Rhea Gilbreath, who grew up in a home in East Tennessee devastated by the effects of World War II. My father, an Air Force pilot, died in action in Europe before I was born and my mother was widowed at twenty-one. She eventually married my dad's best friend who had been on the front lines in France and had returned with shrapnel and shell shock. The three of us were caught up in a tidal wave of emotions and our interactions reflected this. Plus we lived in a community where strict rules about right and wrong, good and bad, led to hefty doses of guilt and shame. Growing up, I felt afraid a lot because I didn't always know how to express my needs or feel it was safe to be myself.

However, there were avenues where I did know how to express myself and where it was safe—playing with my Great Aunt Rose, who saw my inner light and laughed at my jokes, gallivanting with friends, reading, studying and competing for good grades, listening to music and playing in the band, acting in school plays, going to the movies—and this is where the second thread of my story comes in. When I was six, I produced, directed and starred in a neighborhood circus with my friends and "Circus Girl" was born! At sixteen, I entered the Junior Miss Contest and threw myself into a dramatic reading of Amy Lowell's "Patterns," about a woman waiting for her lover to return from war. I lived for the last line, savoring every syllable of *"Christ! What are patterns for?"* and was rewarded for taking the Lord's name in vain by winning first place in talent. Then, while listening to Lizt's "Les Preludes," I was inspired to write down my intention to become an actress who would create works of such truth and beauty that my adoring fans would be swept off their feet. My aspirations were grandiose but I was clear that I wanted to create powerful transformational experiences for others. I didn't know it at the time, but this declaration was my mission statement. I also didn't realize that my mission would be repeatedly sabotaged by the past until I dealt with it.

But not yet. After graduating from Northwestern University, I launched my acting career in New York City and performed in over thirty plays. The pinnacle of this period was appearing in Knoxville, Tennessee, near my home town, as the ingénue in the Broadway Bus and Truck tour of "Butterflies are Free" with Jan Sterling. This culmination of achievements was soon undercut, however, by a swing into depression. It seemed that Circus Girl could only go so high before War Orphan demanded that her needs also be expressed and met. I needed to do a lot of work on myself. Instead, I flew to Los Angeles on vacation.

That was over thirty years ago. I took one look at the Hollywood Hills and that was that...I immediately relocated to Southern California. Within two years, I found my life's work—teaching. I loved helping others express their passion and power and burn their inner lights as brightly as possible. Soon after, I received a Master's Degree in Theater from California State University in Northridge and became a professor of voice and speech at California State University in Long Beach. This new apex of success, however, was increasingly undercut by a horrendous emptiness growing inside me. War Orphan wasn't staying silent.

Fortunately, this time she didn't have to. My life took a new turn when I plunged into a program of trainings, seminars and workshops designed to bring about positive and permanent shifts in the quality of life. They were led by extraordinary world-class speakers and trainers who continue to impact me today. I started taking responsibility for my life, confronting my fears and dropping disempowering patterns. As I was getting in touch with and releasing blocked experiences and limiting decisions from the past, I was also learning how to set my intention, focus myself and produce results—with enormous new freedom and joy. The two threads—War Orphan and Circus Girl—started coming together.

My life began to stabilize. I married, had a son and started teaching and developing courses for UCLA Extension, consulting and giving corporate trainings and coaching business professionals. I also continued to deepen my own personal work. The more work I did on myself, the more effective I grew as a teacher and trainer. It's been like this for over thirty years now—not that it hasn't been chaotic from time to time—but even the chaos has fallen into place inside the bigger picture of my mission—to hold a mirror up to my students' magnificence.

And this brings me to the present: I'm here to share the work I've developed with thousands of students and clients over the past thirty years. My intention is that it provides you with a path to free yourself from the fear of public speaking, to express your passion and your power persuasively, to achieve your intended results and to fulfill the highest aspirations of your heart!

With love and gratitude,
Pamela Gilbreath Kelly
Long Beach, CA
August 30, 2006

Part One

Take Charge of Your Fear

Hooked by the fear of public speaking.

Dismantle Your Fear

"When Demosthenes speaks,
The people say, 'How well he speaks;'
But when Pericles speaks,
The people say, 'Let us march!' "
— Anonymous

We all have an inner Pericles—passionate and powerful, able to inspire people to action. But tapping into this inner Pericles may be easier said than done. Fear of public speaking can get in the way—of taking the spotlight and having people see our flaws—of making a mistake and being criticized.

You may be familiar with the research that states Americans are more afraid of public speaking than of dying. In fact, fear of public speaking tied for first place along with the fear of falling from a great height, while fear of dying was seventh on the list!

The question is, "How do we overcome this fear? What's the key?"

The secret to tapping into our inner Pericles is in making the shift from "fear having you hooked" to "you having fear mastered."

The fear may never disappear completely, but you can take charge of it and control how it affects you. Even megastars like Barbra Streisand and Bette Midler have experienced extreme stage fright before walking into the spot lights of big shows! How can we take charge of our fear the way these celebrities have handled theirs?

Take the Grip Out of Fear

When we're experiencing the fear of public speaking, we move into what's called the "flight or fight mode," which is a state of being driven either to run away from the source of our fear or to attack it. In public speaking, we run away from our discomfort and—to avoid feeling the panic in the stomach or hearing the scream inside the head—we tighten our bellies, breathe rapidly and talk as fast as we can.

Has this ever happened to you? Then when you sat down, you didn't remember what you said or who you saw? It was all a blur! The good news is that all those sensations and inner screams you were running away from are exactly what you want to focus on in order to conquer the fear.

Fear lives in us as body sensations, emotions, thoughts and mental pictures.

By observing each of these manifestations of fear, you will begin detaching yourself from the fear and it will lose its grip on you.

Case Study: ### *Anne Tackles Her Fear of Speaking*

It's powerful to face your fear. About fifteen years ago, I was substituting for another instructor in a course called "Overcoming the Fear of Public Speaking." It was the final session. One of the students was a tall, slender British woman named Anne Reeves, with huge blue eyes and a smile that beamed like the sun. During her final presentation, Anne enchanted us with her warmth, intelligence and animation. She seemed completely natural and was loaded with magnetism!

How Anne felt inside and how she came across!

Imagine how puzzled I was to learn that Anne had no idea how effectively she presented. She was only aware of her anxiety, which had prompted her to take a speaking course in the first place. Since Anne was Director of Marketing for Shimokochi-Reeves, a strategic visual branding company in Los Angeles, she had to give lots of sales presentations, but she vehemently rejected my invitation to take my more advanced course.

Eventually, however, to free herself from her discomfort, Anne did take my course and worked privately with me on her business presentations. But she didn't stop there. Anne joined Toastmasters International and is still going strong! In fact, recently she originated and speaks with other Toastmasters in a presentation about public speaking—aptly called "The Next Level!"

Over time, Anne learned to dismantle and gain control of her fear, allowing her confidence to grow by leaps and bounds. You can too!

How Tension Holds You Hostage

When we're afraid, our muscles tense up and resist gravity. Tension blocks the flow of energy, breath, emotions, thoughts, everything. Tension keeps us stuck with our fear. This is why it's difficult to think on your feet when you're in the throes of public speaking anxiety. And that's why it's easy to blank when you first look out at your audience. The shock shuts down blood to the brain.

The opposite of tension is "releasing to gravity."

Chapter One Exercises

To do the following two exercises, you can read them to yourself as you move slowly through the steps, or you can record yourself reading slowly through the sequences and then play them back, or you can have a friend read them for you.

First we're going to do a relaxation and observation exercise—so that you can distinguish between tension and "releasing to gravity." Take your time and avoid rushing. This exercise may seem long at first, but as you become familiar with it, you'll be able to do a complete run-down for tension in a few seconds. With time and repetition, you'll be able to instantly release your tension if it occurs during a presentation.

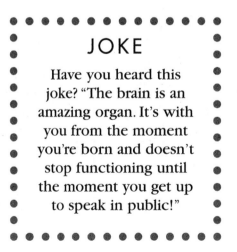

JOKE

Have you heard this joke? "The brain is an amazing organ. It's with you from the moment you're born and doesn't stop functioning until the moment you get up to speak in public!"

Exercise A: Feel the Tension and Release It to Gravity.

- Sit with your arms and legs uncrossed. Let your eyes close. Notice the body sensations in your feet. Notice how your feet are released to gravity.

- Tense your feet. Feel the tension. Now release the feet to gravity. Notice the sensation of release.

- Now do this with your calves. Tense, then release, and notice the sensations of both states.

- Do the same with the thighs—tense, then release, and notice the sensations.

- Then the buttocks—tense, then release, and notice the sensations.

- Move your awareness into your belly. Tense, and notice how hard it is to breathe; then release, and allow yourself to release a big sigh of pleasurable relief.

Feel the tension and release it to gravity.

- Notice the sensations in your chest. Now tense your chest. Notice how shut down you feel. Now release your chest, along with a big sigh of pleasurable relief.

- Bring your awareness into your shoulders, feel them being released to gravity. Now tense them up to your ears. Feel the tension. Then as you release your shoulders to gravity, allow your breath to release as well, with a big sigh of pleasurable relief.

- Move your awareness into your arms. Tense your upper arms. Release. Now tense your lower arms. Release. Tense your hands into fists. Release. Tense your whole arms and hands into fists. Hold. Feel the tension throughout your arms and hands. Now release and feel the release throughout your arms and hands. Feel the release to gravity.

- Now go through these steps of tensing—feeling the tension, then releasing—feeling the release to gravity with your neck, throat, tongue, jaw, eyes, eyebrows and forehead.

By getting familiar with the sensations of "Tense-Release," you're preparing yourself for success if you experience tension—at the podium, in the classroom or during an interview. Simply feel it and release it to gravity!

Exercise B: Observe Body Sensations, Emotions, Thoughts and Mental Pictures

We can break our fear down into body sensations, emotions, thoughts and mental pictures. When we are able to focus on these, we can then release them. Train yourself to notice them and to distance yourself from them when they're not serving your higher goals. How do you do that? Begin when you're relaxed and sitting—perhaps after you've completed Exercise 1. Then read through this next exercise. Again, you can leave your eyes open to read the sequence aloud or you can tape it or have a friend read it to you.

- Close your eyes and release your whole body to gravity.

- Release three big sighs of pleasurable relief, allowing each sigh to bring you into a state of deeper relaxation.

- Now observe your <u>body sensations</u>, beginning with the bottoms of your feet and working slowly up. Perhaps you have some tingling in your right big toe. Or an empty feeling in your stomach. Or some sharp sensation in your left shoulder blade.

- Whatever sensations you feel in your body, observe them and allow them. You are the Observer. You are not your body sensations. You have them. They do not have you. Notice this. Take your time and distinguish your body sensations without resisting them or trying to change them. They are what they are and you are not hooked by them.

- Good. Now sigh your body sensations away with a deep sigh of pleasurable relief.

- Now shift your awareness to your <u>emotions.</u> Observe any emotion that you may be experiencing. Perhaps you feel bored or impatient or peaceful. Perhaps you're experiencing mixed emotions. Whatever emotion you're observing, just notice it, allow it, don't try to change it. You are the Observer. You are not your emotions. You have your emotions. They do not have you. Notice this. Take your time and distinguish your emotions without resisting them or trying to change them. They are what they are and you are not hooked by them.

- Wonderful. Now sigh your emotions away with a deep sigh of pleasurable relief.

- Shift your awareness to your <u>thoughts</u>. Observe any thought as if you were observing a cloud drifting across the sky. You are the Observer. You are not your thoughts. You have thoughts. Your thoughts do not have you. Notice this. Take your time and distinguish your thoughts without resisting them or trying to change them. They are what they are and you are not hooked by them.

- As each thought drifts across your mind, whisper it softly to yourself. You can hear the words of the thought, but you are not the thought. You have the thoughts. They do not have you. The thoughts do not require you to take an action. They are not you. Notice this.

- Now sigh your thoughts away with a deep sigh of pleasurable relief.

- This time, visualize a pleasant <u>memory</u> from your life. See it in your mind's eye as a mental picture. Observe that you have the memory;it doesn't have you. You are the Observer. You are not your memory. Now let it go with a deep sigh of pleasurable relief.

- Now visualize a favorite <u>daydream</u>. Think of something that you would like to happen, but it hasn't actually happened yet. See it in your mind's eye as a mental picture. Observe that you have the daydream; it doesn't have you. You are the Observer. You are not your daydream. Let it go with a deep sigh of pleasurable relief.

- With your eyes still closed, take a moment to review what you have just accomplished. You have distinguished yourself as the Observer. You have observed your body sensations, emotions, thoughts and mental pictures in the form of memories and daydreams. You have them and you're not hooked by them.

- Now release all this with three big sighs of deep and pleasurable relief.

Observe without getting hooked.

As you become more aware of your body sensations, emotions, thoughts and mental picture (memories and daydreams), they lose their hold. A medical student recently shared with me that he now notices when he's feeling stressed and not only releases the tense muscles, but also identifies the thought that's causing the tension! That's powerful. Now move that ability into a public speaking context and you have someone who can experience fear without being hooked by it. Someone who is free to *speak with passion, speak with power and get the results they want!*

Case Study: I Wrestle with My Thoughts

When I gave my very first corporate training in Los Angeles, I noticed a potentially deadly monologue inside my head. The trainees and I had come back from lunch and, as I was delivering the training, I looked out at their faces and thought, "They look bored. They're not getting value." Immediately I started feeling panicky and thought, "I'm a failure."

At that moment, I realized that I was hooked by my thoughts and judgments. So I let them go and began running an entirely different conversation in my head. "They love this training. This is what they look like when they're getting value. I'm a success!" (Keep in mind that this was happening in nanoseconds as I was simultaneously giving the training.) My flagging spirits revived, the training was a success and my evaluations for the training were great! If I hadn't spent years practicing this kind of awareness, I would have been lost in a downward spiral of defeatist thinking!

I changed a downward spiral into an upward spiral.

Summary

The more you practice releasing tension and dismantling your fear, the more freedom you'll have when you're speaking. Instead of being hooked by any fearful body sensations, emotions, thoughts and mental pictures that might occur, you'll recognize them for what they are and take charge of them.

Notes:

_____

_____

_____

_____

_____

_____

_____

_____

_____

CHAPTER 2

Vanquish Inner Losers and Claim Your Fame

"Don't worry about failure.
Worry about the chances you miss
when you don't even try."
— Unknown

In addition to dismantling her fear, Anne Reeves also grew unwilling to be a victim of fear any longer.

To be hooked by fear is to be a victim of fear. Think about it. When we're afraid, what happens physiologically to our bodies? The blood rushes from the extremities and towards our vital organs. We turn ashen and the heart pounds. The body appears to shrink, the shoulders hunch, the chest caves and the arms cross in front. We seem to wither on the vine.

This body language is the typical victim posture. It's also the body language of a frightened little child. When you're deeply into your fear of public speaking, how old do you feel?

Case Study: Little Pam Faces Her Bad Results

I'm reminded of being six and my first-grade teacher made me stand outside the classroom door because I had colored in someone's coloring book without asking permission. I recall that the school principal walked down the hall towards me and I tried alternately to be invisible, to pretend I was going for a drink of water and to put on a nonchalant face. He was probably amused, but I was in a pickle—victimized by my classmate, my teacher and now by the principal! Of course, the truth is that I had put myself in that position.

Years later, while standing before an audience to speak, I was reminded of this incident and felt waves of embarrassment and guilt. Suppressed experiences have a way of suddenly emerging when we're in the spotlight. It's no wonder that some of us run the other way.

Recognizing the Inner "Valerie Victim"

I can't tell you how many times I've watched unprepared students winging their presentations, floundering painfully and coming up with all kinds of excuses for not being prepared. As long as they're getting mileage out of their excuses, they're stuck in a "Valerie (or Vince) Victim" role and their speaking suffers.

It's not my fault if I'm not prepared!

But when these same students take responsibility for their results, they buckle down, do the work, develop their skills and grow their success. They own their passion and power, lay claim to their greatness and audiences love them for it!

In the following exercise, I'll ask you to answer questions designed to uncover the limiting, self-sabotaging Valerie (or Vince) Victim patterns, as well as her strengths.

Exercise A: Remember a Time When You Felt Victimized

(Write or speak your answers.)

• Go back as far as you can remember. How old were you?

• What happened?

_____

_____

_____

_____

_____

_____

_____

_____

_____

_____

_____

- What were your body sensations and emotions? Thoughts and mental pictures?

_____

_____

_____

_____

_____

_____

_____

_____

_____

- What were you unable to communicate or express to someone? What is it about this experience that you did not get acknowledged for?

_____

_____

_____

_____

_____

_____

_____

_____

- Did you make decisions about being a victim? What were they (e.g. being unloved or unlovable, unwanted, stupid, alone, nothing, not enough, etc.)?

_____

_____

_____

_____

_____

_____

_____

_____

- When and how has this episode replayed throughout your life?

_____

_____

_____

_____

_____

_____

_____

_____

_____

_____

_____

_____

- How has this pattern served you? What has it allowed you to get away with (e.g. getting to feel sorry for yourself, playing it safe, hiding, etc.)?

_____

_____

_____

_____

_____

_____

_____

_____

- How has this pattern cost you? What opportunities for growth have you denied yourself (e.g. turning down an opportunity, life lacks adventure, etc.)?

_____

_____

_____

_____

_____

_____

_____

_____

_____

_____

_____

_____

• Are you willing to let these limiting memories, decisions and results go? Please read aloud <u>boldly</u>, *"I release these memories, decisions and results now!"*

• Notice if any body sensations, emotions, thoughts and mental pictures come up and write (or speak) about them here. If you have a lot of emotion, keep going through this section until it lessens.

_____

_____

_____

_____

_____

_____

_____

_____

• Are you willing to be the adult that you are, to do what works and be accountable for your results? Please read aloud <u>boldly</u>, *"I am willing to be the adult that I am, to do what works and to be accountable for my results."*

• Notice if any body sensations, emotions, thoughts and mental pictures come up and write (or speak) about them here.

_____

_____

_____

_____

_____

_____

_____

_____

_____

- Congratulations! As the Observer, you have distanced yourself from the limitations of Valerie–Vince Victim. Since you are no longer identified with being a victim, what could you stand for that inspires you (e.g. getting a better job, going back to school, volunteering)?

_____

_____

_____

_____

_____

_____

_____

_____

_____

_____

- Now look at the flip side of Valerie–Vince Victim. What are her strengths? Compassion and empathy? Good listener? Sense of humor? What else? List them here.

_____

_____

_____

_____

_____

_____

_____

• These are <u>your</u> strengths, they contribute to your passion and your power and they are of value to others. Write or speak 3 assertions about each one of these strengths, referring to being, doing and having (e.g. *"I <u>am</u> compassionate; I <u>listen</u> to others compassionately and with empathy; I <u>have</u> compassionate and loving relationships."*).

_____

_____

_____

_____

_____

_____

_____

_____

_____

• Read each of these statements with conviction. Read them gazing into your eyes in the mirror, projecting your voice and putting your heart into it. Continue doing this until you believe yourself and are owning the statements fully. Note your body sensations, emotions, thoughts and mental pictures below.

_____

_____

_____

_____

_____

_____

_____

_____

Good job! Through awareness, we expose limiting childhood decisions and, instead of being jerked around by them, we can choose to do what works. We can also claim our fame by owning our strengths and recognizing that they are of value to others. Now let's look at another common sabotaging pattern.

Recognizing the Inner "Butch Bully"

The other side of the child-victim role is the parent-judge role. We might cling to an inner victim because we have a bullying inner judge—a "Butch Bully" who holds us to the highest standards and won't let us get away with anything less than absolute perfection!

Often in my trainings, speakers become overly apologetic when they take a sip of water, clear their throat or correct a mispronunciation during their presentation. This is counter-productive. Who wants to sit through a speaker who is overly apologetic about being alive? When you give yourself permission to be human, so will your audience. They want a flesh and blood person owning their power, speaking with passion and leading by example.

Next are other questions for you to answer. These will help expose and eliminate Butch (or Betty) Bully's impossible standards, while maintaining his valuable strengths.

You will be perfect or else!

Exercise B: What are Your Impossible Standards?

(Write or speak your answers.)

- What are they (e.g. Do you have to be liked, perfect, funny, right, in control, impressive, smarter, richer, better, younger, sexier, thinner, what?)?

_____

_____

_____

_____

_____

_____

_____

_____

_____

_____

- How do these standards get expressed in what you say when you're interacting with yourself and with others?

_____

_____

_____

_____

_____

_____

_____

_____

_____

- How do these standards get expressed in how you come across? Your body language and voice?

_____

_____

_____

_____

_____

_____

_____

_____

_____

_____

_____

• When you are hooked by these standards, what are your body sensations, emotions, thoughts and mental pictures?

_____

_____

_____

_____

_____

_____

_____

_____

_____

• What is your earliest memory of this pattern? How old were you? What happened?

_____

_____

_____

_____

_____

_____

_____

_____

_____

- What were your body sensations, emotions, thoughts and mental pictures?

_____

_____

_____

_____

_____

_____

_____

_____

- What were you unable to communicate or express to someone? What is it about this experience that you did not get acknowledged for?

_____

_____

_____

_____

_____

_____

_____

_____

_____

- What decisions did you make at the time?

_____

_____

_____

_____

_____

_____

_____

_____

_____

_____

- When and how have these decisions played out through your life?

_____

_____

_____

_____

_____

_____

_____

_____

_____

_____

- How has this pattern served you? What has it allowed you to get away with (e.g. being arrogant and angry, dominating self and others, etc.)?

_____

_____

_____

_____

_____

_____

_____

_____

_____

_____

- What has been the cost? How has this pattern held you back (e.g lack of love and acknowledgement, failed opportunities, etc.)?

_____

_____

_____

_____

_____

_____

_____

_____

_____

- Are you willing to let these decisions, patterns and results go? Read aloud <u>boldly</u>, *"I willingly release the bully decisions, patterns and results now!"*

- Notice your body sensations, emotions, thoughts and mental pictures and write (or speak) about them here.

_____

_____

_____

_____

_____

_____

_____

_____

_____

_____

_____

- Are you willing to be the adult that you are, to do what works and be accountable for your results? Read aloud <u>boldly</u>, *"I am willing to be the adult that I am, to do what works and to be accountable for my results now!"*

- Notice your body sensations, emotions, thoughts and mental pictures and write (or speak) about them here.

_____

_____

_____

_____

_____

_____

_____

_____

_____

_____

_____

_____

- Congratulations! As the Observer, you have distanced yourself from the limitations of Butch–Betty Bully. If you are no longer identified with his impossible standards, what could you stand for that inspires you (e.g. getting a promotion, buying a boat, running for office)?

_____

_____

_____

_____

_____

_____

_____

_____

- Now look at the flip side of Butch Bully. What are his strengths? Focus and energy? Persistence? Attention to details? What else? List them here.

_____

_____

_____

_____

_____

_____

_____

_____

_____

_____

- These are <u>your</u> strengths, they contribute to your passion and your power and they are of value to others. Write 3 assertions about each one of these strengths, related to being, doing and having (e.g. *"I <u>am</u> persistent and unstoppable; I <u>focus</u> and <u>persist</u> until the goal is accomplished; I <u>have</u> great results because of my persistence)."*

_____

_____

_____

_____

_____

_____

_____

_____

_____

- Read each of these statements with conviction. Read them gazing into your eyes in the mirror, projecting your voice and putting your heart into it. Continue doing this until you believe yourself and are owning the statements fully. Note your body sensations, emotions, thoughts and mental pictures below.

_____

_____

_____

_____

_____

_____

_____

_____

_____

Summary

Facing up to our inner Valerie–Vince Victim and Butch–Betty Bully means bringing awareness to what does and doesn't work. By confronting the pay-offs and costs, we free ourselves from their limitations. Then we can own our strengths and recognize the value these are to others. In fact, these strengths are part of our magic!

Listen to what Anne Reeves has to say now.

"What's made the biggest difference, through the experience of preparing and delivering presentations and confronting my fear, is that I've come to accept myself. I used to have no tolerance for myself; I couldn't allow myself to have weaknesses or to just be mediocre. I always had to be perfect. So of course I was uptight and afraid! Now, I accept what I do well and what I don't do so well. I realize that I have assets others don't have and vice versa. My advice is to avoid trying to be something you're not and to capitalize on what's great about you!"

Straight from the horse's mouth!

Notes:

_____

_____

_____

_____

_____

_____

Reprogram Your Fear

*"Whether you think you can
Or you can't, you're right."*
— Henry Ford

An Overview of Traditional Hypnosis:

Interview with Hynotherapist, Michael Almaraz

Some individuals choose hypnosis to help them overcome their fear of speaking. When I asked hypnotherapist and former client, Michael Almaraz, of Deeper States Hypnotherapy, to explain how hypnosis works, he responded with characteristic gusto. "The hypnotist leads the client into a state of deep relaxation, in which the filter separating the conscious and subconscious minds disappears. It is then possible for the hypnotist to plant suggestions in the client's subconscious mind that will allow the client to start losing their fear of speaking and replacing it with confidence and enjoyment."

Michael has not only helped his clients overcome their fear of speaking, but several years ago, he hypnotized himself to reprogram his fear about giving seminars. As you read through the steps he took, imagine yourself taking them.

The Steps of Hypnosis

Step 1: Achieve Deep Relaxation

"In a relaxed position and with eyes closed, I imagine I'm standing at the top of a staircase and slowly I lead myself down, one step at a time, counting from ten to one. Every step I take leads me into a deeper state of relaxation. To test my relaxation, I must be unable to lift my leg. If I'm able to lift it, I go back to the top of the stairs and begin descending again. When I'm unable to lift my leg, I know the filter separating my conscious and subconscious minds has vanished and I'm ready to receive suggestions."

Step 2: Make Suggestions

The following are Michael's suggestion to himself; however, you can easily translate them to your own specific needs.

- "<u>I remind myself</u> about how much I love being a student of hypnosis and sharing it with others."

- "<u>I tell myself</u> that I'm completely focused on giving away my knowledge and helping my audience."

- "<u>I recall</u> that there are really only two states—pain and pleasure—and I'm here speaking to ease people's pain and replace it with pleasure."

- "<u>I affirm</u> my own pleasure—the relaxation in my muscles, my love of hypnosis, my burning desire to help others."

- "<u>I assert</u> that I feel these in my body and in my emotions as extreme pleasure."

> **TIP**
>
> Record yourself reading suggestions like these and play them back while relaxing or sleeping

Traditional hypnosis entails these two states of relaxation and suggestions. When Michael is deeply relaxed in the pleasure state, with his subconscious mind fully receiving his suggestions, he then goes outside traditional hypnosis. He plants visualizations, or pictures, and physical triggers as well.

Step 3: Add Visuals

Michael adds visualizations to his suggestions:

- "<u>I see</u> myself looking relaxed and confident."
- "<u>I notice</u> my audience appearing enthusiastic and engaged."
- "<u>I picture</u> my audience easily responding as I lead them into hypnosis."
- "<u>I observe</u> them sharing excitedly about their experience of hypnosis."

Step 4: Plant Triggers

Michael also plants tactile triggers, such as feeling a rush of powerful emotions as soon as he enters the room or touches the lectern.

- "I feel a burst of confidence the moment I step towards the front of the room."

- "I experience a rush of excitement when my hand touches the lectern."

By adding visualizations and tactile triggers to his auditory suggestions, Michael feels that he accelerates the reprogramming process. After this "total immersion," he slowly brings himself back to an alert state.

As a result of his self-hypnosis, plus working with me on the content and organization of his seminar, Michael reprogrammed his fear of speaking. Not only that, but he unexpectedly discovered he loves speaking and giving seminars. Now Michael creates as many opportunities as possible to share his ability to replace his clients' pain and fear with pleasure and confidence!

Nontraditional Hypnosis–Psychoneurolinguistics:

Interview with the Author of "Keying: The Power of Positive Feelings", Dr. Donald Dossey [1]

I first met international phobia expert, Dr. Donald Dossey, after reading his book "Keying: The Power of Positive Feelings." In it, Dr. Dossey laid out a powerful strategy for eliminating phobias. I contacted him to order his book for my students and we ended up becoming good friends, which is easy to do with this big bear hug of a man! Recently, I interviewed him for this book.

Dr. Dossey has helped reprogram many individuals suffering from public speaking phobia, or *"specanophobia."* He explains, "What I do is change them from one hypnotic state to another one. You know how a cartoon hypnotist will give someone a post-hypnotic suggestion to cluck like a chicken every time they hear their name? When my clients first come to me, they act as if they've been given the post-hypnotic suggestion to get scared every time they have to give a talk. This is the worst thing that can happen."

"To be an effective speaker, you can't be caught up in your own feelings. You have to be able to focus outside yourself and to notice the feedback you're getting. So what I do is change the post-hypnotic suggestion. Instead of 'get scared' when you have to speak, I reprogram it to 'feel calm and relaxed,' 'be alert' and 'enjoy yourself.'"

The "Think–Feel–Do–Have" Success Strategy

The process that creates success is the "think–feel–do–have" motivation strategy. What you think, you begin to feel; then feeling moves you into doing and doing produces what you have or become. This cycle is interrupted by the fear of public speaking, or by any phobia, for that matter. Thinking ("public speaking") causes the feeling (fear) and then the fear causes the thinking ("I'm afraid of public speaking!") and the vicious cycle of "think–feel–feel–think" is set into motion. To help his patients get off this destructive merry-go-round, Dr. Dossey uses two approaches: (1) <u>Keying</u> to change the feeling and (2) <u>Refocusing</u> to change the thinking.

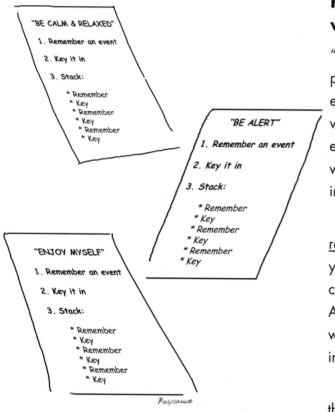

"BE CALM & RELAXED"

1. Remember an event

2. Key it in

3. Stack:

* Remember
* Key
* Remember
* Key
* Remember
* Key

"BE ALERT"

1. Remember an event

2. Key it in

3. Stack:

* Remember
* Key
* Remember
* Key
* Remember
* Key

"ENJOY MYSELF"

1. Remember an event

2. Key it in

3. Stack:

* Remember
* Key
* Remember
* Key
* Remember
* Key

Raycasso

How to Lock in Good Feelings with Keying

"Keying" refers to a simple reflex conditioning process of locking in the feelings you want to experience and locking out the feelings you don't want to experience. This process is done through easy gestures, such as touching your left knee, wiggling your right big toe or bringing your left index finger and thumb together.

So let's say you want to feel <u>calm and relaxed</u> when you have a presentation. What you do first is recall any experience of feeling calm and relaxed (e.g. while getting a massage). At the height of those feelings, you key them in with your chosen gesture (the key), such as holding your left wrist or wiggling your right big toe.

To make these feelings more intense, repeat this process by remembering other instances of feeling calm and relaxed, and then keying them in, using the same gesture. Dr. Dossey recommends this repetitive layering technique, which he calls "stacking."

Next, suppose you also want to feel <u>alert and in a peak performance state</u>. You recall an experience when you felt like that (e.g. playing tennis) and, because you want these feelings to also influence your speaking, you use the same gesture to key in the feelings.

For public speaking, you also want to key in the feelings of <u>enjoying yourself and having fun.</u> So remember times when you had these good feelings and use the same gesture to key them in.

Again, you may have to "stack" each state by layering the experiences and keying them in each time. Then use your key each time you think about, practice and deliver your presentation—to lock in the desirable feelings and lock out the undesirable feelings.

You can also key in any desirable state whenever you spontaneously experience it in life. Whether you're relaxing in the spa, being alert while biking or enjoying yourself watching a football game, key it in!

How to Refocus Your Thoughts and Shift out of Fear

In addition to locking in good feelings with physical keys, you can also shift yourself out of the "think–feel–feel–think cycle" by refocusing your mind. Here are some refocusing techniques Dr. Dossey uses to help his patients conquer *"specanophobia."*

REFOCUS YOUR THOUGHTS

1. Change yourself

2. Run movies

3. Rerun movies

4. Future-pace

5. Up close, loud, strong

6. Reframe

- Change yourself: When you're giving a presentation, if you suddenly feel afraid, change what you're doing. Examples of this are eye-connecting with someone different in the audience, moving away from the lectern, walking towards someone, gesturing, speaking louder or asking a question. By changing yourself, you change your state.

Case Study: Dr. Dossey Appears on Oprah

Dr. Dossey vividly recounts being interviewed by Oprah Winfrey. It was the year her show jumped to number one on the networks. "I was in the green room freaking out! There were all these celebrities waiting to go on, there were millions of viewers, my mind was racing and, being an interna-

tional fear expert, I recognized terror! I remember jumping, stretching, running, pacing, anything to break that 'think–feel–feel–think' cycle! I was also using my most powerful key, remembering a time when I was a little boy and had made my mother proud of me by turning cartwheels. 'What a good little boy I am to make my mother so proud!' The refocusing and keying enabled me to be interviewed by Oprah on the very show that sent her ratings over the top!"

Dr. Dossey had keyed in his
most powerful memory.

• What are your most powerful memories? Write them here and be sure to key them in.

More ways to refocus your thoughts:

- Run Movies: While keying in good feelings, also "run movies" of yourself giving your presentation in the future. See yourself looking like you're having fun, hear yourself sounding alert and confident and feel yourself being calm and relaxed. *The subconscious mind isn't aware of past, present or future and responds as if it's all real, ordering your behavior to produce those results.*

- Rerun Movies: While keying in the good feelings, rerun memories of speaking experiences you've had in the past. Inject these memories with the calm, relaxed sensations; the alert, peak-performing feelings and the sense of having fun. You will be rewriting your personal history by remembering them "as if" you were masterful. The subconscious mind responds with, "Yes you are!" Memories are rewritten and future actions fall correspondingly into place.

- Future-pace: See yourself already having accomplished your goals. Hear yourself talking about how successful you are and feel how capable and powerful you are. Your subconscious mind will then order your behavior to be consistent with the "think–feel–do–have" strategy you fed it.

Case Study: An Olympic Runner Creates His Edge

The winning runner set his course with future-pacing.

Dr. Dossey shared about an Olympic runner who used future-pacing to win his race. As he was squatting on the starting line, the runner visualized himself at his home, after the race, telling his family about how he won. He saw, heard and felt his family's elation. By creating this possibility, the runner focused on his desired future, overcame any fear that could have interfered and won the race. Future-pacing gave him the competitive edge.

- Up Close, Loud and Full-Strength: While you're running or rerunning movies and future-pacing, bring the images up-close so they become large. Turn the volume up loud and pour in strong feelings. This intensifies the messages received by the subconscious mind, which will then guide your actions to achieve those results.

- Reframe: When thinking and feeling about speaking, use words that expand, rather than limit, your possibilities for success. The word "fear" is problematical, but "horse-race nerves" is exciting. "Problem" limits possibilities, but "challenge" opens them up. "Dread" throws on a wet blanket, while "anticipate" motivates.

　　　Now it's time for you to try out these tools.

Exercise A: Lock in Good Feelings with Keying

- Remember and write below a time when you felt calm and relaxed. Bring the visual images up close. Turn up the volume and when the feelings are strong, key them in with a physical gesture, such as touching your left knee.

- Stack the key by remembering and writing other experiences of feeling calm and relaxed and keying them in. Use the same gesture.

_____

_____

_____

_____

_____

_____

_____

_____

_____

- Repeat this process with experiences of feeling alert and peak performing. Use the same gesture.

_____

_____

_____

_____

_____

_____

_____

_____

_____

_____

_____

- Repeat this process with experiences of feeling a sense of enjoyment and fun, using the same gesture.

_____

_____

_____

_____

_____

_____

_____

_____

_____

Exercise B: Refocus Your Thoughts

- Future-pace by visualizing yourself after giving a great presentation. Where are you? Is anyone else there? What are you talking about? How are you feeling? Be specific and write your answers below. Now bring the images up close, turn up the volume and heighten the feelings.

_____

_____

_____

_____

_____

_____

_____

_____

- Run a movie of yourself giving a presentation. Key in one state at a time as you run through the presentation—calm and relaxed, alert and peak performing and experiencing fun. If you start to feel twinges of fear, stack that key and rerun the movie. Note any elements you want to remember.

_____

_____

_____

_____

_____

_____

_____

_____

_____

_____

- Write down your limiting beliefs about public speaking and reframe them. For example, I've often heard students exclaim, *"I just want to get this over with as fast as I can!"* Because their brain receives this emotional command, the student then proceeds to speed through their presentation in record time, leaving their listeners in the dust, wondering what was said. By becoming aware of the problem, the student can notice the fearful thought and replace it with *"I'm excited to share my information with my audience!"*

_____

_____

_____

_____

_____

_____

_____

_____

_____

_____

_____

_____

_____

_____

- How would you reframe this statement? *"I'm uptight at the beginning and afraid I'll blank, but once I get into it, I'm fine!"* [2]

_____

_____

_____

_____

_____

_____

_____

_____

_____

_____

_____

_____

_____

Summary

Through the keying and refocusing techniques, Dr. Dossey has made it possible to interrupt the automatic "think–feel–feel–think" fear pattern and replace it with the "think–feel–do–have" motivation strategy. When you apply these tools, you can reprogram the fear of public speaking into the fun of public speaking!

Both Dr. Dossey and Michael Almaraz demonstrate the power of mind over matter: "If I can think it, I can be it!"

Notes:

_____

_____

_____

_____

_____

_____

_____

_____

_____

_____

_____

_____

CHAPTER 4

Discover Your Big Purpose

"Whatever you can do, or dream you can, begin it.
Boldness has genius, power and magic in it. Begin it now."
— *Goethe*

It works to have a purpose larger than ourselves. A big purpose allows us to shift the focus off ourselves and onto something that inspires us, whether it's having a career that we love, providing for our family or running for office. Having a big purpose puts our fear of public speaking in perspective, which opens the door to clarity and wisdom.

Playwright and political activist, George Bernard Shaw, wrote these stirring words about his big purpose. Read his words aloud, allowing the passion and the power behind the words to flow through you.

"This is the true joy of life, the being used for a purpose recognized by yourself as a mighty one; the being a force of nature instead of a feverish selfish little clod of ailments and grievances complaining that the world will not devote itself to making you happy. I am of the opinion that my life belongs to the whole community and as long as I live it is my privilege to do for it whatever I can.

I want to be thoroughly used up when I die, for the harder I work the more I live.

I rejoice in life for its own sake. Life is no 'brief candle' to me. It is a sort of splendid torch which I have got hold of for the moment, and I want to make it burn as brightly as possible before handing it on to future generations." [3]

Take Back Your Power

To see your life's purpose as clearly as Shaw saw his requires unwavering commitment. Native American wisdom teaches that our clarity and power are trapped within our attachments to possessions, relationships and endeavors. Fear is a symptom of these attachments. Our life's work is to free ourselves from these entanglements, making enormous power available to us.

An easy way for you to begin this process is to look for the messes in your life and clean them up. For instance, is there clutter in your home or workspace? Are there unpaid bills or bounced checks? What about unresolved upsets in your relationships? Do you carry around painful memories from events that happened years ago? When we clean up each of these areas, fear is replaced by clarity and the power to create a joyful, purposeful life.

The following exercise is meant to be done over time and not all at once. Commit to making a workable plan to take consistent actions and notice how fear turns into energy, clarity and confidence.

Exercise A: Clean Up Your Life [4]

(In each category, make a list and cross out items as you complete them.)

• Organize, clean and repair your home, clothes, workspace, automobile, possessions.

- Balance your checkbook.

- Pay past bills or make new agreements.

_____

_____

_____

_____

_____

_____

_____

_____

_____

- Handle broken agreements. Acknowledge them and make new agreements.

_____

_____

_____

_____

_____

_____

_____

_____

_____

_____

_____

- Clean up any lies, including half-truths; return any stolen or "borrowed" items.

_____

_____

_____

_____

_____

_____

_____

_____

_____

- Resolve any upsets, either by eliminating the source of the upset or by being responsible that you don't get upset.

_____

_____

_____

_____

_____

_____

_____

_____

_____

- Deliver all undelivered communications, in person, by phone or by letter. Take responsibility for your interpretations and avoid playing the blame game (Valerie–Vince Victim and Butch–Betty Bully play the blame game).

_____

_____

_____

_____

_____

_____

_____

_____

_____

- Get complete with your body, by handling broken agreements and making new ones, resolving upsets, delivering undelivered communications and cleaning up lies or half-truths.

_____

_____

_____

_____

_____

_____

_____

_____

_____

Continue working through the steps in this book and while you're cleaning up your life, move on to this next exercise.

Exercise B: What is My Big Purpose?

(Write or speak your answers)

What do you want your speaking to contribute in the areas below? Let yourself go and write down or speak your wildest dreams. Write down everything you want to <u>be, do and have</u> in the areas below.

• Your personal life? Who do you want to be? What do you want to do? What do you want to have?

_____

_____

_____

_____

_____

_____

_____

_____

• Your professional life? Who do you want to be? What do you want to do? What do you want to have?

_____

_____

_____

_____

_____

_____

_____

_____

_____

_____

- Your friends and family? Who do you want to be? What do you want to do? What do you want to have?

_____

_____

_____

_____

_____

_____

_____

_____

_____

_____

- Your organization? Who do you want to be? What do you want to do? What do you want to have?

_____

_____

_____

_____

_____

_____

_____

_____

_____

- Your community? Who do you want to be? What do you want to do? What do you want to have?

_____

_____

_____

_____

_____

_____

_____

_____

_____

_____

- Your nation? Who do you want to be? What do you want to do? What do you want to have?

_____

_____

_____

_____

_____

_____

_____

_____

_____

- Your planet and the universe? Who do you want to be? What do you want to do? What do you want to have?

_____

_____

_____

_____

_____

_____

_____

_____

_____

- Do you see a theme emerging? Perhaps it has to do with continually growing and being more, challenging yourself and doing more, stretching yourself and having more. Put your theme into words that inspire you and write it here.

_____

_____

_____

_____

_____

_____

_____

_____

Maybe your big purpose needs to evolve over time and reveal itself to you. If so, then live in the questions, "What is my big purpose in life? What am I up to? What am I building?" And keep coming back to these lists.

When you have a presentation to give, rather than being hooked by fear, focus on your big purpose.

Review of Part One

At this point, whether you have worked your way through some or all of Part One, you have taken a bite out of your fear of public speaking. Perhaps you've dismantled it and have become aware of tension and how to release it. You're distinguishing and releasing fear sensations, emotions, thoughts and mental pictures. Maybe you're reframing and reprogramming your fear. Or you've begun to recognize and free yourself from the limiting patterns of Valerie–Vince Victim and Butch–Betty Bully. Then again, you could be cleaning up your life and discovering a bigger-than-life purpose that inspires you and puts your fear in perspective. The point is, you're beginning to have the fear, instead of the fear having and hooking you.

So when your boss comes to you and says, "I need you to give a presentation in two weeks," you can respond, "You got it!" Now it's time for the rubber to hit the road. It's time for you to take the actions that lead to a presentation you and your boss will be proud of.

Part Two

Take Simple Steps Consistently

Practicing with a mirror and tape recorder.

CHAPTER 5

Ask the Right Questions

"Ask and it shall be given to you;
Seek and you shall find.
Knock and it shall be opened to you."
—Matthew 7:7

Years ago, I read a popular book called, "Zen in the Art of Archery."[5] In it, the Zen Master teaches his student, the archer, that to be successful, he must not only be the archer, but he must become the arrow and the target as well! This is true of speaking too. In order to become a successful speaker, you must expand beyond your usual habits of thinking and responding. By asking the right questions, you get this process underway.

Questions to Ask Right Away

• How much time do I have between now and when I give my presentation?

The answer to this question tells you how much time you have to prepare. This is the first step in developing your *time line*, a plan for preparing, practicing and polishing your presentation. We'll explore the time line in the next chapter; but for now, remember that you want to begin your preparation as soon as possible. By the way, Valerie Victim doesn't ask this question *("Why bother when you can wait until the last minute and then really suffer?")* and Butch Bully won't let you enjoy the process *("You will follow the time line within an inch of your life, or else!")*.

• How much time do I have for my presentation?

It is a rare speaker who stays within or under the time allotment. Don't be a "wind bag." Do you want your audience wishing you would drop through a trap door in the floor? Then heed the words of the famous Parisian fashion designer, Coco Chanel, "Less is more!" Your audiences will be grateful.

- What is the purpose of the event in which I'm presenting?

- Am I appearing with other speakers? What are their topics?

Always look for the big picture to tie into. If your presentation is one of several at a conference, then know how it fits into the whole, so you can tie into the theme and move the program forward with vigor. If you're among a line up of speakers and you know their topics, you can refer to the other speakers as well.

- What is the purpose of my presentation? What do I want my audience to take away with them?

> **TIP**
>
> To speak clearly, you must have a clear target.

In "The 7 Habits of Highly Effective People," Stephen Covey advises us to "Begin with the end in mind."[6] Effective results begin with intention. What response do you want? Do you want to change your audience? How? Do you want them to take an action? What? What idea do you want your audience leaving with?

Susan B. Anthony Asks for a Vote

In her 1872 speech advocating women's right to vote, Susan B. Anthony provides a shining example of clear speaking and a clear target. Read her introduction and conclusion aloud to witness her laser focus.

"...I stand before you tonight under indictment for the alleged crime of having voted at the last presidential election, without having a lawful right to vote. It shall be my work this evening to prove to you that in thus voting, I not only committed no crime, but, instead, simply exercised my citizen's rights, guaranteed to me and all United States citizens by the National Constitution, beyond the power of any State to deny..."

"…Webster…define(s) a citizen to be a person in the United States, entitled to vote and hold office. The only question left to be settled now is: Are women persons? And I hardly believe any of our opponents will have the hardihood to say they are not. Being persons, then, women are citizens; and no State has a right to make any law, or to enforce any old law, that shall abridge their privileges or immunities. Hence, every discrimination against women in the constitutions and laws of the several States is today null and void…" [7]

Susan B. Anthony spoke clearly into her target.

Questions to Ask about Your Audience

• Who is my audience? Are they homogeneous or mixed?

• Do they know more than I? Less? Same? Mixed?

• Why are they coming? What does my audience want to take away with them?

Every audience is different, which means your target is always different. When I'm preparing for a training, I like to have the participants fill out questionnaires before-hand, describing the purpose of their presentations and who their audiences are. Their responses provide me with rich information for tailoring the trainings.

> ### TIP
> When you're preparing, know who you're speaking to. You don't want to confuse a mixed audience by using insider jargon and jokes or annoy an experienced audience with beginner information.

- Does my outcome overlap with my audiences' outcome?

- What do I want my audience to see, hear and feel as they observe me speaking? What do I want them thinking about me?

Make it easy on yourself. Plan to give your audience what they're coming for. For instance, a city engineer spoke at a community gathering of citizens who were disgruntled because a construction project was blocking traffic in their neighborhood. They were at the meeting to learn when the construction would end and the engineer's job was—not to sugar coat the truth so they could walk away happy—but to give them the factual answer.

A former student and client is a prolific speaker and has an effective approach. When she books a presentation, Dorothy Breininger, CEO of The Center for Organization, always asks her client what is the number one outcome they want that will make her presentation successful.

Questions to Ask about Your Set-up

- Where will I be speaking? How large is the room? What is the setting? Is there a stage? A stationary lectern with a microphone?

- What time of day? Where am I in the line-up of speakers?

> ### TIP
> If you're unfamiliar with the room you'll be presenting in, do yourself a favor and scope it out. Walk around, get comfortable in it, test the acoustics, and practice your presentation in it as much as you can.

- How many will I have in my audience?

- What is the best way to stage my presentation?

It aids your preparation to have a picture of the space in your mind, so you can start preparing yourself to fill it with your energy and voice.

Questions to Ask About Staging Your Presentation

- Do I have flexibility about audience seating? If so, would a horse-shoe arrangement work better than theater seating? Or will everyone be sitting around a conference table?

- What's the best placement for my projector so it doesn't block someone's view?

- Will I need a lectern?* A microphone? How much space do I have to move around in?

> **TIP**
>
> Also, if you're one of several speakers, you want to know as soon as possible if you're going to be the first speaker after lunch or the last speaker of the day, so you can make sure you do what works—keep it energetic, use humor, involve your audience, cut it short and finish early.

Asking these questions helps you establish the _big picture_, deal with the specific circumstances and clarify intention. Giving a weekly meeting to the same audience is different than introducing a new policy to all departments, or honoring a retiring employee at a holiday party or speaking to the community about an unpopular topic. A sales presentation to busy decision-makers is distinct from a project review in which you're asking for more time and money. By accounting for these differences, you're on your way to giving a powerful presentation.

> ***NOTE**
>
> Many people refer to the lectern as a "podium", which is actually a platform. It works for me as long as we're all on the same page.

Questions to Ask About Your Effectiveness

- Do I want my audience to see me looking relaxed and enthusiastic? To hear me sounding confident? To feel my sincerity?

Ask yourself these questions early in your preparation. The answers become part of your purpose. Also ask yourself what you want them to be thinking:

"He's prepared. I feel relieved."

"She knows what she's talking about. I'll ask a question."

"He's organized. I'm going to take notes."

"She's not wasting my time. I'm confident in her."

These questions are potent motivators for you to do what works—prepare and rehearse. They cause you to stretch past your usual patterns of thinking and to expand what you're accountable for. These questions increase your chances of success!

This next question reveals our yardstick for success.

• What does it mean to be an effective communicator?

First, notice that we're talking about "communicating," which encompasses but is not limited to public speaking. Communication could be between two people, in person, on the phone, on-line and involves both speaking and listening.

What do you think it means to be effective? Does it mean to speak clearly and concisely? To be understood? To use active listening? It could, but not necessarily. *To be effective is to produce your intended result.*

Extraordinary result-producing communicators, which includes public speakers, share these four characteristics:

The Four Distinctions of Extraordinary Communicators [8]

1. Effective speakers have clear targets

Effective speakers set outcomes by <u>visualizing</u> themselves achieving and having their intended results, by <u>thinking</u> about their outcomes "as if" they are already successful in achieving them, and by <u>feeling</u> a burning desire and sense of expectancy. This is the inner work that must accompany your preparation and rehearsal.

Dorothy Breininger, who co-wrote "The Time Efficiency Makeover," [9] shared with me recently that setting outcomes is actually a time management tool. For instance, when she's going to be attending a seminar, she decides in advance to sit in the front row and to meet the speakers. During the breaks, she makes a beeline for them. Her system works and Dorothy has developed professional relationships with several notable authors, speakers and celebrities. Like Dorothy, you can manage your time by setting outcomes to achieve your goals.

Martin Luther King Asks for a Dream

When Martin Luther King spoke in front of the Lincoln Memorial in 1963, he inspired the nation with his vision, burning desire and sense of expectancy. Read his words aloud and experience the passion and the power of his inner preparation.

"I have a dream that one day on the red hills of Georgia the sons of former slaves and the sons of former slave owners will be able to sit down together at the table of brotherhood.

I have a dream that one day, even the state of Mississippi, a desert state sweltering with the heat of injustice and oppression, will be transformed into an oasis of freedom and justice.

I have a dream that my four little children will one day live in a nation where they will not be judged by the color of their skin but by the content of their character." [10]

2. Effective speakers take in the feedback

Effective speakers have sharp senses, are receptive and read their audience's responses as they speak—drinking them in through their eyes, ears and sense of touch. How can you know if you're being effective or ineffective if you're not aware of your audiences' reactions? Do they look alert and engaged? Do you hear fidgeting, whispering, sighing? Does the energy feel thick and static or alive? You must be able to read your audience.

What makes this sensory acuity possible is preparation. A prepared speaker is free to take in audience response through their senses. Valerie Victim, on the other hand, who waits until the last minute to prepare, is too frantic to notice the feedback; and Butch Bully, who prepares within an inch of his life, is too tense. Both are closed circuits.

> ### TIP
> When you have a presentation to prepare, harness the same powers that Martin Luther King did. Visualize yourself having your intended outcome; think about your outcome "as if" it is already yours; and feel a burning desire and sense of expectancy as you prepare and rehearse. (In Chapter 3, Dr. Donald Dossey refers to this as "future-pacing.")

TIP

Develop your ability
to read your audience
by preparing yourself,
so you don't have
to be thinking about
what to say.

3. Effective speakers have flexibility

When a speaker's senses tell them they're not producing their intended result, then they must shift gears and continue shifting gears until they are effective.

Flexibility involves altering what you're saying and how you're expressing yourself. Examples include picking up your energy, inviting more participation, increasing voice projection and vocal variety, moving out from behind the lectern, slowing down and speaking more clearly, pausing, getting to the point, providing more examples to back up your assertions, using more humor, taking a stretch or water break. The more speaking you do, the more adept you become at making these adjustments with ease.

Benjamin Franklin Asks for a Constitution

Benjamin Franklin demonstrated strong sensory acuity and subtle flexibility in his speech at the Constitutional Convention of 1787. He was talking to the most powerful leaders in the United States, with differing ideas about what should be contained in the Constitution. Take your time as you read his words aloud. Move beneath the unfamiliar language and experience his exemplary radar as he navigates among the political egos of his listeners.

"...Thus I consent, sir, to this Constitution, because I expect no better, and because I am not sure that it is not the best. The opinions I have had of its errors I sacrifice to the public good... Much of the strength and efficiency of any government, in procuring and securing happiness to the people, depends on opinion, on the general opinion of the goodness of that government, as well as of the wisdom and integrity of its governors. I hope, therefore, for our own sakes, as a part of the people, and for the sake of our posterity, that we shall act heartily and unanimously in recommending this Constitution wherever our influence may extend, and turn our future thoughts and endeavors to the means of having it well administered. On the whole, sir, I can not help expressing a

wish that every member of the convention who may still have objections to it, would, with me, on this occasion, doubt a little of his own infallibility, and, to make manifest our unanimity, put his name to this instrument. "[11]

4. Effective speakers send congruent messages

Effective speakers communicate their message through what they say and also through how they express themselves. When words, body language, voice and inner commitment and conviction are in harmony, the speaker's message is *congruent*. The opposite is termed a *mixed* or *incongruent* message.

Ben Franklin navigated with exemplary radar.

Occasionally I work with clients who have something important to say in their business presentations, but they smile too much, or shift their weight back and forth, or speak in a weak, wispy voice. These behaviors send a mixed message about their confidence and credibility. Likewise the speaker who looks polished and professional, but misuses or mispronounces words or clutters his speaking with *"uh's"*, *"like's"*, *"okay's"* and *"you know's."* Or what about the speaker who is dressed inappropriately or is unkempt? All these kinds of signals are inconsistent with the intended purpose and are blatant tip-offs that the speaker is unprepared, unaware or unskillful. When it's your turn to speak, eliminate the verbal clutter, master definitions and pronunciations and make sure your appearance is consistent with and not distracting from your purpose.

If this is starting to sound like Butch Bully speaking to you, think of it this way. Self-correcting is *choosing* to eliminate whatever is inconsistent with your intended results; it's not *obsessing* about being perfect. And the elimination process takes place <u>over time</u>, not over night.

• How can I come across congruently and avoid sending mixed messages?

Think for a moment about how your audience receives your message—through their eyes, ears and sense of touch. Your listeners see your eye contact, facial expression and body language, as well as your mouth shaping the words. They also hear your words and your voice tone and tempo. And they feel your energy and emotions, which are expressed through commitment and conviction. Altogether, these make up the four languages you must harness.

The 4 Languages of Public Speaking: The 4 V's

VERBAL: What you say—the words, ideas, data, information

VISUAL: How you use your body–eye contact, facial expression, posture, gestures, movement (visual aids, props and video)

VOCAL: How you use your voice tone and tempo (recordings and music)

VISCERAL: How you use your commitment and conviction

When the 4 V's are all working in harmony together, you are sending a congruent message.

Exercise: Project Congruently

Time to take action! We're going to practice congruency with three statements that represent three desirable attitudes you would want to express in a presentation—(1) enthusiasm, (2) confidence and (3) sincerity.

1. *"I'm glad to be here!"*

2. *"I know what I'm talking about!"*

3. *"I care about what I'm saying!"*

You're going to express each of these statements congruently. Do this in the mirror or with a partner. Feel free to change the words to suit your personal style. For instance, to avoid sounding belligerent with #2, you could say *"I've done my research and I know my facts."*

Also you may want to think of specific situations that would motivate each statement. This is called *personalizing.* To motivate enthusiasm, for instance, you could imagine that you're at a reunion and your listener is your best friend from high school.

• First, express each statement with your <u>body language only</u>, without saying the words. Stand up and use your eyes, face, gestures, posture, movement, all of your body.

• Next, express each statement with the <u>words and your voice only</u>, without using any facial expression or body language.

- Now, express each statement with <u>everything—the words, body language, voice </u>and make sure you're pouring your <u>emotions</u> into the ideas.

- Last, express each statement again with everything and <u>be ten times bolder and louder.</u>* Be over the top, but pour your emotions into the ideas. This rehearsal technique pushes you beyond where you usually stop yourself. Enjoy the freedom.

Case Study:
Angelo Faces a Large Audience

It pays to ask the right questions. One of my clients, the CEO of an investment company, needed to give a presentation at an international conference with eight thousand people! As we worked together on his content and style, in the back of my mind, I was worried about having him be ready to deal effectively with so many people. For days, I searched for the answer to how could Angelo prepare himself for eight thousand people? Speaking to my classes or to a Toastmasters' meeting wouldn't provide a large enough scale to prepare him. But the Pacific Ocean would! So I asked Angelo to start practicing at the beach, speaking to the ocean AS IF his breath, words and ideas were causing the ocean to ebb and flow and the winds to blow. He agreed and loved the experience of tapping into the power of the ocean. Inspired, he drove his family to the mountains and practiced speaking to the mountains AS IF he were causing them to rise towards the sky. Next, he went to the Hollywood Bowl when no one was there except a custodian and he spoke from the stage to thousands of empty seats. At this point, Angelo felt ready. Not only was his presentation a success, but as he was speaking, he felt comfortable enough to walk from the stage and into the aisle to be closer to his audience!

*NOTE

"Be ten times bolder and louder." This is where some speakers balk. They feel phony and self-conscious and exclaim "I'm an engineer (or whatever) and would never talk like this! I'd lose all credibility!" They're right. "Ten times louder" is a <u>rehearsal technique only </u>which frees us from fear-based "Butch Bully" concerns (e.g. "I must be perfect!") that suppress our personality, passion and power.

*Ask the right questions to expand
your possibilities.*

Speaker, speaking and purpose became one. By asking the right question, a solution was found and Angelo was ready for his audience— of eight thousand!

Summary and List of Questions for Future Presentations

When it's time for you to begin preparing a presentation, you'll boost your rockets by asking and answering these powerful questions. Here is a list of all the questions from this chapter. I recommend that you make copies of this list to have for all your presentations.

Questions to Ask Right Away

• How much time do I have between now and when I give my presentation?

_____

_____

• How much time do I have for my presentation?

_____

_____

• What is the purpose of the event in which I'm presenting?

_____

_____

• Am I appearing with other speakers?

_____

_____

• What are their topics?

_____

_____

- What is the purpose of my presentation?

_____

_____

- What do I want my audience to take away with them?

_____

_____

Questions to Ask about Your Audience

- Who is my audience?

_____

_____

- Are they homogeneous or mixed?

_____

_____

- Do they know more than I? Less? Same? Mixed?

_____

_____

- Why are they coming? What does my audience want to take away with them?

_____

_____

- Does my outcome overlap with my audiences' outcome?

_____

_____

- What do I want my audience to see, hear and feel as they observe me speaking?

_____

_____

- What do I want them thinking about me?

_____

_____

Questions to Ask about Your Set-up

• Where will I be speaking?

_____

_____

• How large is the room?

_____

_____

• What is the setting?

_____

_____

• Is there a stage?

_____

_____

• A stationary lectern...?

_____

_____

• ...with a microphone?

_____

_____

• What time of day?

_____

_____

• Where am I in the line-up of speakers?

_____

_____

• How many will I have in my audience?

_____

_____

- What is the best way to stage my presentation?

_____

_____

_____

Questions to Ask about Staging Your Presentation

- Do I have flexibility about audience seating?

_____

_____

_____

- If so, would a horse-shoe arrangement work better than theater seating?

_____

_____

_____

- Or will everyone be sitting around a conference table?

_____

_____

_____

- What's the best placement for my projector so it doesn't block someone's view?

_____

_____

_____

- Will I need a lectern? A microphone?

_____

_____

- How much space do I have to move around in?

_____

_____

Questions to Ask about Your Effectiveness

- Do I want my audience to see me looking relaxed and enthusiastic? To hear me sounding confident? To feel my sincerity?

- How will I make this happen?

_____

_____

_____

_____

_____

_____

_____

_____

_____

- What does it mean to be an effective communicator? How will I produce my intended result and give the audience what they're coming for?

_____

_____

_____

_____

_____

- How can I come across congruently and avoid sending mixed messages?

_____

_____

_____

_____

_____

_____

- What other questions do I have?

_____

_____

_____

_____

_____

Notes:

_____

_____

_____

_____

_____

_____

_____

_____

_____

_____

_____

Make a Plan
The Time Line

"First things first"
— *Stephen Covey*

We build homes and send probes into deep space according to plans. No matter how much or how little time you have to prepare for your presentation, start right away by making a plan or *time line*. In a similar way that an outline gives you points to cover in a particular order, the time line lays out the steps you must accomplish as you move towards your presentation. Also remember the purpose of your time line and the purpose of your presentation is to achieve your intended result. So what does your time line need to cover?

What the Time Line Covers

- First, it needs to take into account all of <u>the time you have to prepare.</u> Whether you have minutes, days, weeks or months—take advantage of all of it. Dr. Roy Meals, a hand surgeon with The University of California, in Los Angeles (UCLA), took one of my courses because he wanted to start preparing for his farewell speech as President of his professional society, which was 2 1/2 years away! At the end of this chapter, you can read Dr. Meals' account of his preparation for this address.

- Second, your time line must include <u>specific dates by when each step will be started and completed.</u> *I recommend beginning with the date of your actual presentation and then scheduling the steps backwards.* What needs to be handled the day of the presentation? The day before? Two days before and working backwards to today's date? I have found this approach to be very realistic and effective.

- Next, account for these steps of preparation (these are listed in chronological order):

    1. Ask the right questions about audience, purpose and logistics (Chapter 5).

    2. Build a container for your ideas with a mind map, outline and note cards (Chapter 7).

    3. Pour in the juice with practicing and polishing (Chapter 9).

    4. Develop and practice with visuals (Chapter 10).

    5. Prepare for questions and answers (Chapter 11).

- Then, break these larger categories down into smaller steps:

    1. Develop your introduction, body and conclusion (Chapter 7).

    2. Enhance with cohesives, hooks and connectors (Chapter 8).

    3. Do run-throughs of the whole presentation.

    4. Practice being congruent and fully associated (This relates to body language, voice and "pouring in the juice", which we'll cover in Chapter 9).

    5. Make a final check-list (Chapter 10).

    6. Preview and practice in the room where you'll be presenting.

    7. Arrive early to your presentation.

> **TIP**
>
> By arriving early to your presentation, you can get set up and then be free to greet and meet people as they arrive. When it's time to begin your presentation, they're not strangers and you're warmed up!

Case Study: Dr. Meals Shares His Time Line

Here is Dr. Roy Meals' account of his 2 1/2 years preparation for his farewell address to the American Society for Surgery of the Hand. It demonstrates his commitment over the long haul to being the best speaker he could be. As you read it, put yourself in his shoes and experience his determination.

- *Fall 2001: Began thinking about what I could mention in my presidential address that would be unique and meaningful.*

- *January 2002: Took "Public Speaking for Professionals" through UCLA Extension. Ten-week course, as I recall. Instructor, Pam Kelly, at end encouraged us to continue improving our skills by joining and participating in Toastmasters.*

- *April 2002: Visited the ballroom where my presidential address would be given, which allowed me to visualize myself there during my preparation.*

- *Spring 2002–Spring 2003: Attended Toastmasters, gave the ten speeches required to become a Competent Toastmaster (CTM).*

- *Summer 2003–Spring 2004: Continued with Toastmasters, giving speeches that tried out ideas, some of which would become part of my presidential address.*

- *May, June, July 2004: Drafted and revised speech and developed no more than twenty PowerPoint slides that embellished and illustrated the major points of my outline. Listened to Toastmaster audiotapes while jogging: winning speeches from their annual international contest as well as famous speeches from Martin Luther King, John Kennedy, Winston Churchill.*

- *August 2004: Met weekly with speech coach, Pam Kelly. Very valuable. Tightened logic and flow, improved analogies, improved timing, gestures, inflection. Most of all, improved confidence.*

- *Late August, 2004: Practiced the speech walking to work and while taking long bike rides. Also daily practice with my dog as audience. Great for practicing sustained eye contact!! I let the meeting planners know that I wanted to have a cordless lavaliere mike and a remote PowerPoint controller available for the meeting.*

- *Early September, 2004: Stopped constant practice. Ran through speech no more than once a day.*

- *September 8, 2004: Dress rehearsal in the ballroom with stage lighting, lavaliere mike, remote Power-Point controller.*

- *September 9, 2004: Gave speech to approximately 2200 hand surgeons from around the world. Mission accomplished! Preparation well worth the effort. I had fun. I was relaxed and confident. People to this day continue to congratulate me and recognize my efforts in preparation and delivery. The succeeding Presidents have recognized that the bar has been raised regarding what our members consider an acceptable presidential address.*

- *Sequel: I now actually enjoy public speaking and look forward to opportunities to use the hard earned skills of eye contact, gestures, voice modulation, etc, to persuade an audience.*

Dr. Meals' time line reveals the power of setting outcomes and taking consistent, committed actions over time.

Before and After: focused on content vs. focused on connecting

No Time for a Time Line?

For you who think you have no time to prepare and practice, time-management expert Dorothy Breininger has two powerful questions for you to ask yourself every day before your presentation.

- What is the one thing I can do today that will make the biggest difference?
- How many minutes do I have to work on my presentation today?

And then you answer the questions and take action. You'll notice all excuses dropping by the wayside.

Summary

When you make a time line for your preparation and rehearsal, you're powerfully in action, bringing your intention to life by laying out a plan for the successful completion of your presentation—meaning that both you and your audience will get to go home satisfied.

Now let's go to work on that timeline!

Time Line:

Begin with the date of your presentation and work backwards to today's date.

What are your goals for each day?

_____

_____

_____

_____

_____

_____

_____

_____

_____

_____

_____

_____

_____

_____

_____

_____

_____

_____

_____

_____

_____

_____

Build a Container for Your Ideas
Structure and Content, PREP, Mind Mapping, Outlining

"Let thy speech be better than silence;

or be silent."

— Dionysius

Often when we first begin preparing and speaking out loud about a topic, we tend to ramble, use too many words and tell everything we know. To paraphrase Abraham Lincoln, *"If you want a twenty-minute speech, I'll need two weeks to prepare it. If you want a two-hour speech, I'm ready right now!"* We come across more professionally when we distill and structure our ideas. Luckily, we have formulas that make this process easy.

In 500 BC, Aristotle wrote that a good tragedy has a beginning, a middle and an end, and his formula has dominated Western literature ever since. Said another way, who hasn't heard of *introduction, body and conclusion?* And then there's the world-renown speakers' organization, Toastmasters International, which refers to structure this way: *"First you tell them what you're going to tell them. Next you tell them. Then you tell them what you told them!"* This structure is in our DNA and you can count on your audience to listen for it.

The Three Rungs for Building the Container for your Ideas

(You'll need notecards)

Think of these steps as rungs on the "Container Ladder." Each rung takes you towards the top, where you will then step onto another ladder. This first rung trains you to get to the core of your message.

Rung 1: Cut to the Chase with the PREP Formula [12]

Point – Reason – Example – Point

Here are two examples. Read both aloud several times, throwing yourself into each. This first PREP is based on the presentation a planner gave at The Southern California Association of Governments. I've added some wishful thinking of my own.

P – Did you know, our Southern California air quality is better than it's been in years!

R – Because of the decisive actions we've been taking.

E – First, we've developed and implemented cleaner fuels at the pumps. Then there's a surge in hybrid sales and a renewed commitment to car and van pooling. Finally, we have thousands more people taking advantage of our rapid transit and riding bikes and motorcycles to work.

P – Taken all together, in Southern California, we're seeing farther and breathing easier because, when the solutions were presented, we took action!

Notice how the PREP formula leads you to the essential facts of the message so you don't waste words. The opening Point presents the main idea, which is paraphrased in the closing Point. The Reason offers a broad statement about why we're seeing change and the Example captures the components of this change (Actually, I gave three examples).

I used this next PREP for a training with Thai Airlines.

P – You must experience Thailand, the incomparable jewel of Asia.

R – Because Thailand offers you the riches of history and the pleasures of the modern world.

E – Picture yourself in the exotic storied capital of Bangkok; then having easy access to historical sites and cultural wonders throughout this spectacular country. Imagine yourself enjoying some of the world's most beautiful beaches, underwater scenery, golf courses and luxurious spas—all making Thailand an irresistibly romantic destination!

P – These are just some of the reasons why Thailand is the incomparable jewel of Asia…and why you must experience it for yourself!

Although the language is picturesque and exuberant, the PREP structure demanded that I stick to the heart of the message.

The PREP formula is useful when you begin preparing your presentation. It provides you with a structure and forces you to clarify and distill your ideas to their essences. No wind bagging here!

Recently, I taught the PREP formula to foster youths who were learning to make requests of social workers and judges on their own behalf. After practicing with each other, several youths volunteered to stand in front of their peers and deliver their PREPs. Here's a dramatic example.

P – I request to be returned to my biological family.

R – Because they are no more violent and abusive than my foster family.

E – If I were with my biological family, at least I could see my brothers and sisters, look after them and help my parents out.

P – Since my biological parents are no more abusive and violent than my foster family, it would make a big difference to me and I would be happier if I could live with my biological family.

By compressing her request into the PREP formula, the young speaker became powerful and unforgettable.

Exercise A: Prepare, Practice and Present a PREP.
(You'll need notecards)

Step 1: Write a PREP

Write a PREP about a hobby. Why a hobby? Because you'll enjoy speaking about it! Don't try to be brilliant. Keep it simple. For example:

P – I love running.

R – Because when I run, I feel great all day.

E – For instance, after running in the morning, I can produce results all day long without having to stop and rest.

P – That's why I'm a runner and I love it!

Now it's your turn.

_____

_____

_____

_____

_____

_____

_____

_____

_____

_____

- Also write a job-related PREP.

_____

_____

_____

_____

_____

_____

_____

_____

_____

_____

_____

_____

Step 2: Mind to Mouth

- Now choose one of these to practice out loud.

- Read it out loud. Does it sound like you?

- Change it until it sounds natural and conversational.

- Then *explain* the ideas until they flow.

Step 3: Make it Yours *(Use notecards)*

- Write only the key words on a note card.

- Practice on your feet with the note card, *explaining* the ideas until they flow.

- Eliminate *"uh"*, *"like"*, *"okay"*, *"you know"* and other verbal clutter.

- Now eye connect with a partner or with yourself in the mirror.*

- Stay eye connected and practice *explaining* the ideas to your partner or to yourself in the mirror.

> ### TIPS
>
> When you <u>explain ideas</u>, you connect to your listeners. When you focus on remembering words, you break that connection.
>
> ———
>
> To use notecards effectively, become accustomed to glancing down at your notecard and allowing the words to trigger the ideas. Then look back up and connect with your partner or with yourself in the mirror as you explain the ideas.

Step 4: Project Congruently

- *Stand tall and explain* your PREP with <u>enthusiasm</u>. Use your eyes, face, gestures, voice and emotions.

> ### *NOTE
>
> Sometimes when students begin combining eye connection with speaking, they become discombobulated and the ideas fly right out of their brains. This is natural and, if it happens to you, rest assured that this tendency will subside and eventually disappear <u>with practice</u>.

- Next, *explain* your PREP with <u>confidence</u> and use everything you've got.

- Ditto with <u>sincerity</u>.

- Then, do the same exercise with all three attitudes. (One at a time!)

- Last, do the exercise with <u>ten times more energy and volume</u>.

Step 5: Time Yourself

Anne Reeves frequently tapes herself and then listens to herself as if she's the audience. This lets her hear if the message is coming across clearly and get a sense of the timing. I don't want you to become overly concerned about listening to yourself yet. We'll get to that when we work on vocal techniques. I do recommend that you clock yourself, however, and start developing your sense of timing as you speak.

You have now built a container for yourself, poured in your ideas and delivered your presentation with passion and power! Practice the PREP formula to train yourself to be clear and concise. You can also use it as the nucleus for a longer speech (which we are going to do) or to structure an answer to a question.

> ## TIP
> You can fall back on PREP whenever you're asked to speak impromptu or if the twenty-minute speech you prepared has to be chopped down to one or two minutes because other speakers have wind bagged and eaten up most of your time (Shame on them!).

Now you're ready to climb to the next rung.

Rung 2: Liberate your Brain with the Mind Map [13]

Imagine yourself in a group of writers brainstorming a topic for a speech. One of the cardinal rules is that, at this early stage of preparation, every idea is good and gets written down, whether it's factual or not, and no matter how off-the-wall it sounds. The group will get selective later.

This is the premise of mind-mapping. The difference is that when you're mind-mapping, you're probably doing it by yourself. *Your goal is to empty your conscious mind of all the information and facts you know about the topic and also to draw out of your subconscious mind the free associations, memories, daydreams and feelings which will bring unexpected and interesting touches to your facts. The mind map also uncovers gaps in your knowledge, questions to answer and areas to be researched.*

Now let's go back to when your boss gave you two weeks to prepare a presentation. After asking the right questions about your purpose and your audience, after making a time line and drafting a preliminary PREP, you're ready to *mind map*.

The Steps to Making a Mind Map

- Begin with a blank sheet of paper.

- In the center, write your topic and draw a circle around it.

- Begin brainstorming on paper, drawing circles around each idea and connecting related ideas with lines.

- Bullet all your facts and also explore free associations, including feelings, memories, mental pictures, quotes, music, movies, anything and everything. The more possibilities you come up with, the better. Eventually, you'll separate the wheat from the chaff, but not yet.

- You also want to uncover areas requiring more research.

- Do your research and then plug all the missing information into your mind map.

- When there's nothing more to research; when your mind is totally empty and your mind map is filled with the raw material for your presentation, you're ready for the next step.

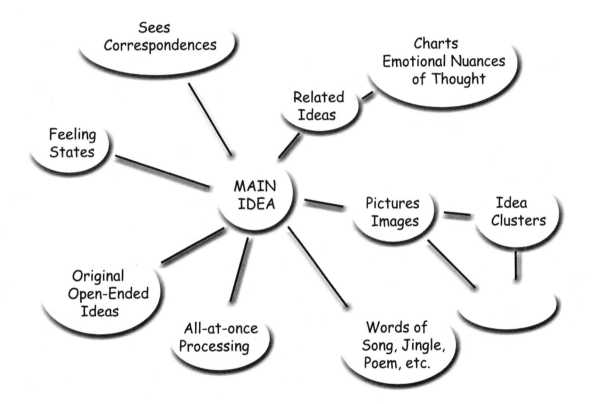

Case Study:
A Planner Uses the Mind Map to Add Interest

Mind mapping helps you uncover the unexpected. A Planner at The Southern California Association of Governments (SCAG) in Los Angeles was preparing to give a report on air quality to elected officials from all over the region. While mind mapping, he recalled a movie title and ultimately decided to use it as his opening attention-getting hook. His presen-

tation was about how air quality in Southern California had improved because of cleaner fuels, car and van pooling and rapid transit (sounding familiar?). His opening attention-getter was "On a clear day, you can see forever!" It got everyone's attention and was a perfect lead-in to his presentation.

Exercise B: Mind Map a PREP

Continue until you come up with at least three unexpected items.

Next, it's time to ascend to the last rung of this ladder.

Rung 3: Bring it Full Circle with the Outline [14]

The last rung is the outline. Your job is to select the best ideas in your mind map and to plug them into the introduction–body–conclusion framework of your outline. This represents a longer, more detailed version of your PREP.

Here's our Planner's outline

I. Introduction

Attention-Getter: "On a clear day you can see forever!"

Preview Statement: "We're not there yet; but because of the actions we've been taking—the cleaner fuels, car and van pooling and rapid transit—we're moving in that direction."

Significance Statement: "We're seeing further and, best of all, breathing easier!"

II. Body/Discussion

Key Point: (one at a time) Cleaner fuels, car and van pooling, rapid transit

Support: Facts and figures, evidence and examples for each key point

Transition: e.g. "So that's how cleaner fuels have impacted pollution. Now let's take a look at the results of using car and van pooling."

III. Conclusion

Review

Thank you

Memorable Statement and Call to Action: "Remember, on a clear day you can see forever! And because of the actions we've been taking, we are seeing further and breathing easier. Now, let's put the pedal to the metal, double our efforts and catch up to that day!"

Exercise C: Prepare and Practice from an Outline.

(You'll need note cards)

Step 1: Bullet an Outline

• Select only the best ideas from your mind map and discard the rest.

• Bullet these ideas (jot down key words only) in the outline that follows. Use the Planner's outline as a model.

• When you've rehearsed enough to be confident about the sequence of ideas, you're ready to bullet your key points onto note cards. But first, I want you to see the whole presentation.

I. Introduction

Attention-Getter:

_____

_____

Preview Statement:

_____

_____

Significance Statement:

_____

_____

II. Body/Discussion

Key Point 1:

_____

_____

Support:

_____

_____

Transition:

_____

_____

Key Point 2:

_____

_____

Support:

_____

_____

Transition:

_____

_____

Key Point 3:

_____

_____

Support:

_____

_____

Transition:

_____

_____

III.Conclusion

Review

_____

_____

Thank you

_____

_____

Memorable Statement and Call to Action:

_____

_____

_____

Step 2: Mind to Mouth

- Practice out loud and on your feet.

- Go through the outline, from introduction to conclusion.

- <u>Explain</u> the ideas until they flow.

- Then explain the ideas to yourself in the mirror or to a partner.

- Time yourself and note the time.

Step 3: Practice from Note cards

- Now bullet your key ideas on your note cards.

- Be sure to clearly number the note cards.

- Practice out loud and on your feet.

- Go through the entire speech, from beginning to end, <u>explaining</u> the ideas until they flow.

- Practice glancing down at your notes, then looking up and connecting with yourself in the mirror or with a partner.

- Go through your speech two times.

- Then be ten times louder and more excited!

- Finally, be yourself, explain and connect.

Good job! Before you step off this "Container Ladder" onto the "Ladder of Enrichment," I want to emphasize that every organization has its own presentation structure and style. Many business presentations, for example, include an agenda of what will be covered, in the introduction.

Adding an Agenda to Your Introduction

What will make your agenda better than the norm is if you capture the critical point about each item. I could say, *"I'll be talking about your verbal message, body language, voice and inner state,"* and it sounds like a grocery list. I risk having my audience tune me out. Or I could include the central benefit about each item to whet their appetite and say, *"First, we'll be discussing how to get our ideas across concisely and clearly; then we'll look at how to use body language to engage our audience; next, how to modulate the voice to reinforce our meaning and, finally, how to personalize our message with our own commitment and conviction."* This is more compelling, don't you think? By the way, I just gave you a preview of enriching the container and pouring in the juice. Remember it for your agendas.

Dealing with Technical Jargon

Every industry has its own language and many presentations are crammed with jargon, acronyms and dense technical language. These provide a quick short-hand for everyone who recognizes them. But you may not have a homogenous audience, so in your early stage of preparation, be sure to ask the right questions. Know who's in your audience and plan to communicate effectively with everyone by speaking a language they all understand.

> **TIP**
> If there's anyone who may not be privy to your organization's technical lingo, then make a point of explaining your jargon and spelling out your acronyms slowly and clearly.

Case Study:
Dorothy Finds Comfort in her Binder

When you have a container for your ideas, you have gravity! You've already been introduced to Dorothy Breininger, CEO of her company, the Center for Organization. Dorothy is a terrific speaker, trainer and seminar leader. Audiences adore her. She's real, funny and committed to contributing to the quality of peoples' lives. But when she first started giving presentations, she was terrified to let go of her script, contained in a large three-ring binder. It was her anchor and she never strayed far from it. Of course, her audiences didn't know this. They were too engaged in her expertise and warm, earthy style. In time, Dorothy internalized her script, became sure of herself and loosened her grip on the binder. But it had served a vital purpose.

Dorothy still has the binder, but is no longer chained to it. She takes her manuscript out of the three-rings and sometimes carries a sheet around as she conducts a workshop. Being the organizational wizard that she is, Dorothy has a key word written boldly at the top of each sheet, so she always knows where she is.

Dorothy used notes to bolster her confidence.

Christine's Mind Map and Speech, "Apples!"

Recently Christine Kurimoto delighted our class with her speech about apples. Notice how her mind map uncovered so many facets of the apple. Imagine what mind mapping could reveal about your job-related topic.

Apples!

Do you know why apples are the best fruit?

Because not only do they taste good, but they're good for you.

Apples are fat-free, cholesterol-free, and sodium-free. They're a great source of fiber and antioxidants. And one medium apple has only eighty calories.

I just heard a story about a bunch of kids at a Catholic school. It's lunchtime, so they all head over to the cafeteria. At the front of the line is a bowl...a huge bowl...filled with shiny, red apples. And next to the bowl, one of the nuns had placed a sign that says, "Take only one. God is watching."

At the end of the line is a tray full of freshly baked chocolate chip cookies...next to which one of the kids put a

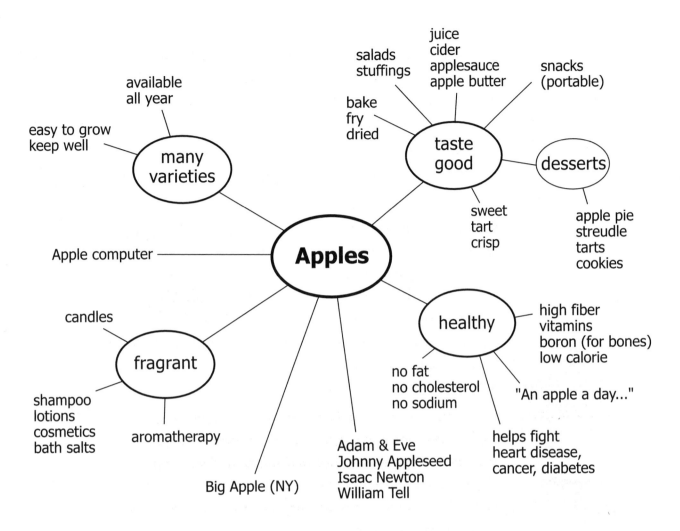

sign that says, "Take all you want. Don't worry...God's busy watching the apples."

Well, seriously, we should all be eating apples as part of a healthy diet.

Recent studies have shown that eating one fresh apple a day has whole-body health benefits, such as reducing our risk of heart disease and cancer...specifically lung cancer, colon cancer and prostate cancer.

The fiber and nutrients in apples can also reduce our risk of stroke, diabetes, and asthma.

Eating two apples a day can lower our LDL cholesterol—which is the bad cholesterol—by as much as 16 percent.

And on top of all that, new studies are showing that the good stuff in apples and apple juice protects our brain cells, which means that it helps fight the damage that can lead to memory loss and Alzheimers, as we get older.

Apples are also great because they're available year-round, they're cheap, and they're versatile.

We all know how portable apples are, which makes them perfect for snacking. But if you don't like eating your apples raw all the time, you can bake them or fry them, poach them, stuff them, or juice them. Apples are wonderful in pies and cakes and all sorts of desserts. And, speaking of desserts... Does anyone here like to bake? Did you know that a good way to reduce the fat and calories when you bake things like cakes and cookies is to replace some of the butter with applesauce?

Other tasty apple edibles are apple chips, apple syrup, apple butter, apple tea, apple wine and even apple soup. You can add apples to salads and salsas, and there's probably a gazillion recipes out there that have apples in them. And, when you cook apples, they don't lose a significant amount of their nutritional value.

So what does all of this mean to us? Well, it means that we really have no good excuse not to get a daily dose of apples.

So, that old saying—and you knew this was coming, right?—that "an apple a day keeps the doctor away" is based on truth. Because apples really are the best fruit!

Summary

While PREP extracts the essence of your message, the mind map yields substance and unexpected pearls and then the outline provides a structure that contains and anchors your presentation. Our next step is to engage the audience more and increase their interest and enjoyment. Time to move on!

Notes:

_____

_____

_____

_____

_____

_____

_____

_____

_____

_____

Enrich Your Container
Cohesives, Hooks and Connectors

"If you show me, I will see;
If you tell me, I will hear;
If you let me do, I will understand."
—Native American Wisdom

At this point, you should be sounding a little like a "talking outline" and perhaps feeling robotic. Not to worry—this is a passing phase in your preparation. You're speaking directly to the point and you're not straying, but your content is "bare bones" and needs to be fleshed out and injected with your personality.

To begin this process, we can add elements to the basic outline that will help make your presentation extraordinary, and we'll do this by first looking at what most appeals to the human brain and to the adult learner.

How the Human Brain Works[15]

The brain is divided into two hemispheres and each hemisphere listens for and responds to different sensations. Effective presentations satisfy each hemisphere.

The Left Brain

- *The left brain is focused on facts and is sequential and analytical. It actively evaluates verbal accuracy, sequencing and vocal confidence. To engage your audience's left brain, you must support your assertions with facts, be easy to track and sound authoritative. When you do this, you gain your audience's confidence.*

The Right Brain

- *The right brain, on the other hand, is holistic. It grasps the big picture all at once and is visual and visceral. It is receptive to verbal pictures, body language and emotion. When you bring these to your presentation, you engage your audience's right brain, their imagination and gain their enthusiasm and sincerity.*

The goal then is to bring the right mixture of left brain and right brain appeals to your audience. Also it helps to understand your audiences by looking at what characterizes adult learners, such as yourself.

How Adults Learn[16]

- *Adults are experienced and knowledgeable.*
  Build on what they already know and find ways for them to contribute, such as by sharing their knowledge and experience.

- *They expect value and immediate practical application.*
  Leave out unnecessary details and "education for its own sake."
  Focus on the "how to's".

- *Men and women want to know why.*
  Tell your audience why they should listen, what your outcome is and what's in it for them.
  Also back up your assertions with facts, not opinions.

- *They need to get the big picture first and to know how the parts relate to the whole.*
  Start with the big picture, cluster information into categories and explain how these categories relate to the big picture.

- *Adults learn by doing.*
  Generate opportunities for participation.

By understanding what appeals to the two hemispheres of the brain and also to the adult learner, you're now ready to step onto the "Ladder of Enrichment." Prepare to climb another three rungs.

The Three Rungs to Enriching your Presentation

Rung 1: Make Tracking Easy with Cohesives

When you utilize cohesives, or sequencing devices, you make it easy for your audience to track you effortlessly and to retain your key ideas. To begin integrating cohesives, ask yourself these questions and make the appropriate changes and additions to your outline and note cards as you go along:

- Did I distill my message into essential points?
  Remember your PREP? Time is valuable and your audience wants practical information that's been boiled down to its essence. Another acronym to remember is KISS, or *"Keep it short and simple"* (also *"Keep it simple, Stupid!"*).

- Did I start with the big picture?
  (As an example and going back to our PREP about Thailand) *"How would you like to wake up with your sweetheart in the most exotic, beautiful and romantic place on earth?"*

- Then did I cluster my information into categories?
  (Example) Three key points: historical sites, natural beauty and recreation

- Have I stated my outcome and benefits up front?
  (Example) *"I plan to convince you to double your efforts to clean up our air! I know you want to eliminate ugly, smelly, toxic smog! Asthma and allergies! And, on top of that, maybe save our planet?"*

- Am I using introductory frames throughout?
  Create an introductory frame for each cluster of information.
  (Example) *"Now we're going to investigate exactly which toxins have been impacted by cleaner fuels."*

- Am I enumerating and using steps and sequences?
  This simple tool makes lists easy to track and remember. Just don't over use it in the same presentation or it will become distracting.

Exercise A: Practice These Cohesives

Punch up each word in the examples below and then pause. In an actual presentation, these words, or "cues," would grab the listeners' attention and they would then hear the point that follows.

> (Examples) "First, next, then, last"
>
> "First, second, third"
>
> "A, B, C"

- Have I backed up all my assertions with support, including statistics, benefits, examples and illustrative stories?
  (Example) *"90 percent of the employees fired last year were let go because of issues related to sexual harassment. You'll find this statistic in this month's Harvard Business Review, Forbes and Money magazines."*

- Am I using transitional, linking and summary statements?
  (Transition) "So that's how car and van pooling have taken a bite out of pollution. Now let's move on to rapid transit and look at its impact."

  (Links, or cues to listen up) "First, next, then, finally;" "yet, but, however, and, nevertheless."

  (Summary) "So taken all together, cleaner fuels, car and van pooling and rapid transit have had a dramatic impact on our air quality!"

- Am I employing repetition and paraphrasing for emphasis?
  State your main message in your introduction, in your conclusion and <u>again after Q and A</u>, as a second conclusive conclusion. Also everything in your body should reinforce your main message. This may feel like over-kill as you're practicing it; but your listeners won't think so, especially if you're paraphrasing your main idea each time.

Exercise B: Add Cohesives to Your Outline and Practice

(Use your notecards)

- Add as many of these cohesive elements to your note cards as you can muster. They will make your presentation, no matter how technical it is, easier for your audience to track.

- Now it's time to practice out loud, using these cohesives. If you're not accustomed to speaking like this, you may feel unnatural and even more like a "talking outline" than you did before. With practice, however, this clear, easy-to-track way of speaking will become habitual and natural. The key is in the practicing.

Step 1: Mind to Mouth

- Rehearse from beginning to end, on your feet, at least three times.

- Use your note cards.

- The first time, just be yourself as you explain the ideas and start becoming familiar with speaking the cohesives aloud.

- Now be ten times louder and more excited as you explain the ideas.

- Finally, be yourself and do it again, this time in the mirror or with a partner. Do it AS IF it's the very first time and you're 100 percent committed to contributing to yourself or your partner.

Step 2: Time Yourself and Note the Time.

What did you notice as you progressed from one run-through to the next? How was the final run-through different from the first? Did you begin to feel more natural and comfortable with this clear, concise, easy-to-track style of speaking? Perhaps not entirely, but somewhat more comfortable? This is good! After all, you want your audience thinking, *"She's prepared. He isn't wasting my time."*

But now it's time to add spices that will liven up your presentation, capture your audiences' imagination and bring in some entertainment value. Let's climb onto the next rung.

Rung 2: Spice It Up with Hooks

We need hooks because minds tune out, drift off or get bored and must be brought back with hooks. Some of these hooks appeal to the left brain and some to the right. Sprinkle them throughout your presentation, beginning with your opening.

A. Rhetorical questions (who, what, where, when, why, how)

(Example) *"Who remembers when gas was under $2.00 a gallon?"*

Remember to pause after your question, and drink your audience in for a brief moment. If someone should actually answer, acknowledge them with eye contact and a brief, warm verbal response before moving on.

B. Dramatic statements

(Example) *"We've seen what happened in New Orleans. If we don't do something about the rate at which we're polluting our atmosphere, Washington DC could be underwater too!"*

C. Startling statistics

(Example) *"Can you believe it? What we say may account for as little as 7 percent of our effectiveness; but how we express ourselves can account for as much as 93 percent of our effectiveness!"*

D. Quotations

(Example) *"Voltaire observed, 'There is only one word for speakers who tell everything they know—boring!'"*

E. Humor

(Example) *"The great philosopher, Raquel Welch, said 'Style is being yourself, but on purpose!'"*

(Example) Karim Jaude, CEO of Dynamics Capital Group, has won several Toastmasters' competitions with a speech about his real-life kidnapping in Beirut during the War in Lebanon in the 1970's. He juxtaposes the harrowing details of being tortured with a touch of humor. When Karim's kidnappers finally release him, after forcing him to sign all his wealth over to them, they allow him to take a few dollars and his American Express card. Karim takes the card out of his pocket, holds it up and banters, *"Never leave home without it!"*

More Hooks:

F. Stories, anecdotes and illustrations

(Example) *"Years of research, development and planning yielded the three key factors that helped us take a big bite out of pollution over a decade ago—cleaner fuels, car and van pooling and rapid transit. Now, pollution is back again and worse than ever. We must come up with more, bigger and better solutions. We did it before. We can do it again. We have to!"*

Karim used humor to lighten the drama.

(Example) Let's say you're giving a speech about how perception determines reality. You could start out by telling a brief story: *"A group of people are sitting around a banquet table laden with the most delicious foods and beverages. But they're all miserable. Why? Because attached to their arms are large wooden utensils. They can't bend their arms to eat or drink and, as far as they're concerned, they might as well be in hell! Then suddenly someone gets an idea. 'Hey! We can't feed ourselves, but we can feed each other!' Now, everyone is feeding the person across from them. They're all talking, laughing and eating and, as far as they're concerned, they are in heaven! Perception determines reality!"*

G. Props

(Example) *One of the speakers in a team presentation for a defense project showed how the pipe his team had developed for a military tank made a critical difference in the Gulf War. He passed around this pipe for all to see up close as he spoke.*

(Example) *In her presentation about public speaking, "The Next Level!", Anne Reeves holds up a dead plant to make the point that, if you don't work on your skills, they wither and die. Her use of the prop is dramatic, humorous and visually memorable.*

H. Actions

(Example) The president of a wire and cable manufacturing company was disgusted with the waste from the previous year. He called all his employees to the auditorium and drove a forklift onto the stage, where he dumped crates representing the waste. *"Actions speak louder than words," and they got the message.*

I. Games

(Example) *Recently a student was giving a sales presentation in class. To get the audience more involved, she had hidden the item to be sold in an attaché case and asked us to guess what it was while she answered our questions about it. This question and answer process drew us into the benefits provided by the hidden object. In a short time, the class guessed the item, which she then revealed, demonstrated and sold. First, she had aroused our curiosity and drawn us in.*

J. Rhymes

With the right audience, rhymes can be memorable. Ads and commercials demonstrate this constantly. When I've used rhymes to introduce myself at networking events, they've made people chuckle and remember me.

(Example)

"Whether you have a toast, a roast,

a presentation or interview of any kind;

If your accent you must reduce;

or your voice must produce... or seduce;

Then step to the front of the line!

I'll help your star to shine.

You'll get your results and that will be fine!

When you talk spam,

it's time to call Pam!

Exercise C: Add Hooks and Practice

(Use your notecards)

- Use both left-brain and right-brain hooks.

- Use a hook as an attention-getter in your introduction. You might start off with a simple rhetorical question for now, and work on developing a more interesting hook later.

- Add a hook to each of your key points in the body.

- Repeat or paraphrase your introductory hook in the conclusion.

Step 1: Mind to Mouth

- Stand and rehearse at least five times.

- Use your outline/note cards.

- At first, just be yourself, explaining ideas, as you become familiar with speaking the hooks.

- Then, explain the ideas and be ten times louder and more excited.

- Next, explain the ideas in the mirror, eye connecting with yourself.

- Now, explain the ideas in the mirror, eye connecting and being ten times louder and more excited.

- Now, just be yourself and explain all your ideas.

Step 2: Time Yourself and Note the Time.

> **TIP**
>
> Since hooks add spice to your presentations, remember to maintain a balance. Too many rhetorical questions, for instance, can become predictable and distracting. Also be sure to choose hooks that are appropriate to your audience and the purpose of the event. Stories, rhymes, games and humor are great when you're speaking to more right-brain groups, such as entertainers or designers. For the more left-brained business, legal or technical audience, choose statistics, props and illustrations that corroborate your assertions. The guiding principle is to be consistent with your purpose of giving your audience what they're there for, so speak their language.

With these rehearsals, is your presentation falling into place and becoming more familiar? Do you need to change the way you're saying something so it feels more natural? Are you feeling more comfortable and perhaps even enjoying yourself at times?

Hooks provide one of the ways we spice up and flesh out our presentations, adding entertainment value to our information. Another way is to add connectors. It's time to step up to the final rung of the "Enrichment ladder."

TIP

Your audience will mirror your inner state and as you confidently assert your statistics, they will be confident in you. When you enthusiastically illustrate a point with a colorful example, they will enthusiastically visualize it with you. And when you pour your sincerity into a heart-felt dramatic statement, your audience will be right there with you.

Rung 3: Establish Affinity with Connectors

How would you describe the experience of *affinity*? As likeness, harmony, understanding? People have different words for describing affinity and these words point to an experience of connection or relatedness. One of the traits of extraordinary speakers is that they are able to establish this sense of affinity with their listeners. How? By appealing to the audiences' three different listening and learning styles.[17]

A. Attract Visual Listeners' Eyes

A large percentage of people are primarily visual. Visual individuals listen and learn predominantly with their eyes and powers of visualization. Look for visual people especially in the arts, design, fashion and beauty fields.

When I gave a training at Sebastian International (now part of Wella) to hair dressers that spoke at large product shows, I was able to be very animated and "over the top" because I was reflecting my trainees' high energy visual style. I would not have gotten away with that at an engineering, accounting or law firm, not if I had wanted to establish credibility and rapport.

Attract Visual Listeners with—

- Illustrative stories and colorful examples

- Visual aids and demonstrations

- Higher energy and enthusiasm

- Higher-pitched, faster-paced voice

- Animated body language and smiling

B. Appeal to Auditory Listeners' Ears

Auditory people listen and learn through their ears and their thinking processes. You'll find them especially in business and fields related to leadership and speaking, such as politics.

Appeal to Auditory Listeners with—

- Logic, facts, statistics, and quotes
- Reading, writing, speaking exercises, word play
- Vocal projection and richness
- Confidence, focus, being in control

Turn back to page 54, and reread Susan B. Anthony's powerful auditory appeal to reason, observing her confidence and focus as she appeals to her left-brained judges who are listening for logic and facts.

C. Connect to Kinesthetic (Visceral) Listeners' Feelings

Kinesthetic individuals listen and learn through their sense of touch and feelings. Like visual listeners, kinesthetic listeners also comprise a large percentage of people. You'll find them especially in the fields of health and social service.

Connect to Kinesthetic Listeners with—

- Human interest stories
- Props
- Role-play
- Sincerity, concern, caring
- Toned-down body language and voice

If you turn back to page 59, and reread Martin Luther King's speech, you will both see and feel his inspirational and moving visual and kinesthetic appeals.

Case Study: Bernard Draws Us In

When I worked with the foster youth in Los Angeles, my co-teacher, Bernard Caliman, masterfully drew in the three listening styles. He had grown up in the foster care system. As he described the story of his childhood, he seemed to relive the fear that had silenced him for so many years and we were under his <u>kinesthetic</u> spell. Then when he recounted being kidnapped and seeing helicopters overhead, his <u>visual</u> images heightened our sense of urgency. However, he also interjected <u>auditory</u> reminders that, as a child, he had not yet learned to let go of the victim role and speak up for himself. The net result? Everyone in the auditorium was completely drawn in to Bernard's story and the lesson he had learned.

Bernard appealed to our senses and drew us in.

By appealing to our three different learning and listening styles, Bernard's presentation was unforgettable. Here's a very different kind of presentation, but equally effective.

Case Study: Lisa Dazzles Us

Pay attention to the details. One of my students, Lisa Colicchio, did just that in her demonstration speech. Lisa made several smart choices. First, she was smart to demonstrate something that she loves—making cupcakes! She further inspired herself by referring to a recipe in her favorite magazine by her favorite guru, Martha Stewart. She didn't stop there. She combined her cupcake activities with informing us about the magazine and why it's her favorite.

Her <u>visual</u> listeners delighted in all the activity—making and spooning batter, icing prepared cupcakes—and in the colorful pages of the magazine, which Lisa had mounted. Her <u>kinesthetic</u> listeners savored the textures and tastes they would soon sample and enjoyed Lisa's warm, nurturing style. Her <u>auditory</u> listeners responded to Lisa's expertise and confidence, as she combined her cupcake activities with informing us about the magazine's different departments. For her finale, Lisa served her cupcakes to the class and gave each person the recipe, which was printed on lovely stationery stamped in glitter with the outline of a cupcake! Lisa had accounted for every detail and captured all our listening and learning styles.

Lisa accounted for every detail and captured our senses!

Technical Presentations Can Appeal to the Senses Too

The same principles apply to more serious business and technical presentations too. Remember the team presentation about the pipe developed for a Gulf War tank? Props, colorful stand-up displays, multiple speakers, vitality and stage movement appealed to all our listening and learning styles.

To Pour in More Data, Empty your Audiences' Teacups

When you want to pour information into your audience, be sure to appeal to their three learning styles. This can make a huge difference. Recently, I attended two 2-day seminars. The first one left me drained and cranky. After the second, I was energized and motivated. Why? Both seminars were loaded with auditory appeals—tons of information and outstanding vocal variety—and colorful slides dominated the visual appeal in each. The speaker in the second seminar, however, broke up the information dumps with an abundance of kinesthetic appeals. These included lots of audience participation, including humor and laughter, interactions and role-playing with audience members, referring to us by name throughout both days, vigorously moving throughout the whole auditorium and having us stand up, stretch and breathe deeply. He also had us sharing ideas with each other and briefly working on projects together. As a result, we felt refreshed, were ready to take in even more information and we left the seminar energized!

If you want to put information into your audience, from time to time, give them opportunities to "empty their teacups!"

Exercise D: Add Connectors and Practice.

(Use your note cards)

- Read through your presentation and notice if you're appealing to all three listening and learning styles.

- If not, then do so. For this exercise, maintain a balance.

- If, however, you're actually giving this presentation to a live audience, appeal to THEIR listening and learning style(s).

Step 1: Mind to Mouth

- Now it's time to explain your ideas, from beginning to end, becoming familiar with the connectors you've added.

- Explain your ideas in the mirror and on your feet.

- Explain your ideas being ten times louder and more excited.

- Now just be yourself and explain your ideas AS IF you're 100 percent committed to contributing to our audience.

Step 2: Time Yourself and Note the Time.

Summary

At this point in your preparation, you've built and enriched your presentation; you're speaking clearly and concisely and are easy to track; you've added hooks to be more persuasive, more entertaining and to capture your audience's imagination; and you've added connectors to appeal to their learning styles. Plus, you have rehearsed your presentation each step of the way! It's becoming more familiar, natural and conversational. Now it's time to jump on the "juice ladder" and to pour in the juice!

Notes:

_____

_____

_____

_____

_____

_____

_____

_____

_____

_____

_____

_____

_____

_____

Pour in the Juice!

Being Fully Associated,
The Two Practice Levels
Body Language, Voice

"Suit the word to the action;

the action to the word..."

— Shakespeare

Extraordinary Speakers Are Fully Associated

We'll breathe passionate, powerful life into your purposeful content by doing what extraordinary speakers do. They are what is called *"fully associated."* The speaking lives in them and they live in the speaking.[18] To get a sense of this, imagine the power of Winston Churchill's words as he stood before Britain's House of Commons when Europe was being threatened by Hitler. Churchill promised, *"We shall defend our island whatever the cost may be; we shall fight on the beaches, landing grounds, in fields, in streets and on the hills. We shall never surrender...."* [19]

Or imagine the passion of Martin Luther King when, in front of the Lincoln Memorial in Washington, D.C., he reached the pinnacle of his dream of true equality, *"Free at last! free at last! thank God almighty, we are free at last!"* [20] Churchill and King poured all the passion and power in their souls into their words. Yes, they each were driven by a big purpose, but you too have a purpose for every presentation you give, class you teach and job you interview for. You too can bring passion and power to your speaking.

How Being Fully Associated Is Different from Congruence

Let's contrast how being fully associated is different from congruence. Your audience perceives your congruent message. If you're expressing enthusiasm, they see enthusiasm in your body language; they hear it in your words and your voice; and they feel it in your energy and emotion, commitment and conviction. *You are congruent in your audience's experience.*

When you're fully associated, it's from you the speaker's point of view. You experience the speaking living in you and you living in the speaking. You speak out of bold inner pictures, bold inner voices and bold inner feelings. If this sounds like acting, it's similar—except you're not pretending to be someone else. You're being yourself, on purpose. But like the actor, you're not talking <u>about</u> your message. You're <u>being</u> your message!

An effective and enjoyable way to access this principle is to share a vibrant personal experience. Then you can more easily apply this experience to job-related presentations, including technical presentations. The following is the speech I give to demonstrate being fully associated:

I Demonstrate the Value in Being Fully Associated

When I was a little girl, I used to have a recurring nightmare about falling off a near-by bridge. Then years later, when I moved to the South Bay, I would be driving home on the Harbor Freeway. You know that exit that seems to go way up into the sky? I would see that and start panting with fear—as if I were up there about to fall!

Given my fear of heights, why in the world, years later, am I standing on the edge of a cliff preparing to jump? Because I'm doing a ropes course called the zip line. I'm standing on a narrow little diving board; my arms are extended above my head and my hands are wrapped around a handle bar that fits over a rope. This rope is the zip line and it's tied to a tall pine tree behind me. Then this rope comes down at an angle... down... down... down... to the ground, where it's anchored. Around it are these tiny little people who are waiting for me to jump and come zipping down the rope where they'll catch me.

The instructor is behind me and she says, "OK, Pamela, lean forward and push off with your feet!" I can't move. I'm frozen with fear. I can only hear a voice screaming inside my head, "No! This can't be happening!" The instructor knows just what to do. She changes her tone and bellows, "Do I have to tell you again? I said lean forward and push off with your feet!" It works. I do what she says, close my eyes, lean forward, push off with my feet and scream. Now I'm careening down the zip line and screaming bloody murder!

Suddenly, the wind blows up my body, my eyes open and I realize, "This is fun!" I start swinging back and forth, squealing and showing off in front of those tiny little people at the other end of the rope... who are getting bigger and bigger and bigger...until... Boom! I'm on the ground. They're helping me out of my harness. The tears are streaming down my face and I'm saying over and over, 'I did it! I did it! I did it!"

How did I do it? The last thing I remember is that I'm on that little diving board, frozen with fear.

Here's what I've come up with. As long as I stayed frozen on that little diving board, my fear was bigger than me. It had me. But as soon as I jumped— even though I was out of control and didn't know what might happen... at that moment, I had my fear—I was bigger than it. And that has made all the difference.

As I demonstrate being fully associated with this real-life adventure, I act everything out, using lots of body language, voice and emotions. *My purpose is to have my students see what I'm seeing, hear what I'm hearing and feel what I'm feeling. The speaking is living in me and I'm living in my speaking. This is the juice.*

The speaking lives in me and I live in the speaking!

Exercise A: Develop an Entertaining, Fully Associated Speech

Now I want you to share a fully associated personal adventure or embarrassing experience. Next, we'll go through a few steps to structure it into an entertaining speech and then learn some vocal techniques to further "make it pop." Finally we'll look at how to apply this experience to a more reserved, left-brained, job-related presentation.

Step 1: Share an Adventurous or Embarrassing Experience

- Talk AS IF your experience is happening right now.

- Stand up and throw your body, voice and emotions into it.

- Use the present tense.

- Share your story and be fully associated.

Step 2: Develop Your Story

- Focus on who, what, where, when, why, how.

- Eliminate details that don't forward your story.

- Develop sensory details that are visual, auditory and kinesthetic.

- Make sure they move your story forward.

- Run through your story again and be fully associated. Have the speaking live in you and you live in the speaking. Speak out of bright inner pictures, loud self-talk and strong feelings.

Step 3: Develop Your Conclusion

- It's usually easier to develop your conclusion before your introduction.

- Sometimes you need to work through your story or presentation several times to distill it and discover what it's all about. Then you can develop your conclusion and finally your introduction.

- What is the point of your story? Is there a lesson or main idea? If nothing jumps out at you, make it up for now.

- Develop this into your conclusion.

- Practice your conclusion a few times, explaining the idea.

Step 4: Develop Your Introduction

Notice in my zip line story, I concluded with a lesson I learned. When I first began preparing this for my students, my conclusion occurred to me immediately. My introduction, however, which illustrates my fear of heights with brief examples, took longer to prepare and is not the first introduction I tried out. Turn back to pp. 102-104 and review the different ways of hooking. You also might want to experiment with different introductions to find the one that works best for your story.

- Turn your conclusion into an introductory hook.

- Practice your introduction a few times, explaining the ideas.

- First be ten times more fully associated, from beginning to end.

- Then just be yourself—on purpose and fully associated—and do it again.

Step 5: Time Yourself and Note the Time

You now have an entertaining speech, with structure and spontaneity, to share with friends. You created it by moving yourself through two practice levels which you can apply to all your presentations.

Be Fully Associated in Technical Presentations

Before we move into the practice levels, let's consider how you can bring this principle of being fully associated to business and technical presentations.

Remember, the content can be highly technical and filled with numbers, data and acronyms and you can still bring the full force of your personality, including your body language, voice and emotions to your speaking. The numbers, data and acronyms are telling a story and you must commit to being the best story-teller possible.

I suggest that you always fully associate with your commitment to contribute to your audience and with your conviction in what you're saying. And make certain that they can see, hear and feel your commitment and conviction! At the same time, you don't want to risk being "over the top" and losing your credibility. So be fully associated, but also mirror your audience. Stay within their expectations to connect with them and gain their trust. When you have gained their trust, then you can turn up the energy. Whatever the purpose of your technical presentation, when you're fully associated with your commitment and conviction and appropriate to your audience, you will engage them and get the results you want.

Generate Inspiration and Build Stamina

Sometimes speakers expect their audiences to be as committed and fully associated as they are. They expect responsiveness, energy and positive feedback and are thrown off guard when nothing seems to be coming from their listeners. This is natural.

> **TIP**
>
> Train yourself to provide your own motivation and to generate your own inspiration throughout your presentation, from the time you arrive until you depart! Sometimes audiences need time to warm up. Give them a reason by generating your own heat and passion for speaking.

It takes a lot of stamina to be fully associated and to generate your own inspiration. When I first began giving all-day and two-day trainings, I would collapse into bed as soon as possible after each training day. Over time, it became easier and I had energy to spare. So pour your sweat equity into your presentations by being fully associated, generating your own inspiration and building your stamina.

Move through the Two Practice Levels

When you first begin speaking aloud, the juice may not be there. Usually, you'll need to go through stages to fully access your passion and your power. I refer to these as the "Two Practice Levels."

Practice Level One: Explain Ideas Until They Flow

"Explaining ideas" is much different than "remembering words." When you're explaining, you're reaching out and connecting to your listeners—with your words, body language, voice and inner state. It's as if you're saying, *"I want you to see this; I want you to understand this; I want you to be touched by this!"*

When a speaker is remembering words, however, they're a closed circuit, focusing only on their own gray matter, unable to connect with anyone. How many "dry, boring" technical or business presentations have you endured? I've endured many "dry, boring" moments, but then I interrupt the speaker and coach them to connect with one person at a time and explain their ideas. When they do, they're so much more engaging and enlivening!

At Practice Level One, you want to be yourself and talk the way you really talk. On the other hand, to present a professional image, you may need to master your pronunciation of certain words and correct your grammar. These finishing touches are consistent with credibility and have universal appeal.

I also recommend that you practice eye connecting with yourself in the mirror. If you have any timidity about eye contact, mirror work will power you through it.

Practice Level Two: Be Congruent and Fully Associated

Incongruent behaviors are distracting for an audience and dilute the speaker's power. At Practice Level Two, I suggest you practice with a buddy or video/DVD record yourself to see and hear how you're coming across and what adjustments you need to make. The process is like peeling an onion—you become aware of the distracting behaviors and gently let them go, layer by layer.

Have Congruent Body Language

Everything we do and don't do with our body sends a message. We don't want our body language telling the audience that we're suffering from fear, insecurity or lack of preparation or that we're apathetic or exhausted (from staying up all night, like Valerie Victim, preparing at the last minute!). We do want to communicate that we're calm and relaxed, alert and energetic, confident and prepared.

Here are the guidelines for body language I use in my trainings, *as issues come up.* I recommend that you take your time going through them. Read one category at a time and think about each item and why it's on the list.

The Eyes

- Eye connect with individuals in different parts of the room. Avoid predictable patterns of eye contact, such as scanning from side to side, which indicate that you're not really making contact.

- Avoid looking at peoples' foreheads and ears instead of their eyes. This causes a disconnect for you and your audience. Again, if you feel shy about direct eye contact (and different cultures have different rules about it), practice connecting with yourself in the mirror, until you become comfortable.

- Maintain eye contact with one individual for a few seconds, until you experience being connected with them; then move to another person in another part of the room. If you do this, everyone in your audience will experience your being connected to them.

The Face

- Practice having your face express enthusiasm, confidence, sincerity and other emotions appropriate to your presentation.

- If you tone your cheek muscles, your face will look more alive. Lifeless, untoned cheek muscles give the face a blank or hang-dog look. To tone your cheek muscles, just raise and release them several times a day. This will bring energy and life to your face.

  - Smile. A warm, natural smile has magnetism!

  - Also avoid over-smiling, which looks tense and sends a mixed message about preparation, confidence and credibility.

The Arms and Hands

New speakers are often concerned with what to do with their arms. Think about what the arms and hands represent. They allow us to reach out into the world and to give and take, to touch others and express ourselves. How we use our arms and hands reveals how comfortable we are expressing passion and our power to make things happen. When anxious, our gestures tend to look up-tight. When we're relaxed, however, the same gestures have freedom and ease.

- Practice relaxing your shoulders and arms to gravity and gesturing naturally to <u>emphasize a point</u>, <u>draw a picture</u> or <u>express a feeling</u>.

- If relaxing your arms to gravity feels awkward, take every opportunity to practice it. Speakers often hold a pen to lessen tension (just don't play with it!)

- The late President John F. Kennedy has been emulated for his use of gestures at the end of his Inaugural Address, when he emphasized his points with strong chopping gestures, "Ask <u>not</u> what your country can do for <u>you;</u> ask what <u>you</u> can <u>do</u> for your <u>country</u>!"

- Your arms can be hanging relaxed at your sides or one or both bent at the elbows with the hands relaxed. During a performance at the Hollywood Bowl recently, the power of Andrea Bocelli's voice and feelings was augmented by his arms hanging relaxed at his sides.

Self-conscious gestures telegraph anxiety.

- Use the old-fashioned speaker's gesture of touching the ten fingers together in front of the torso with caution. It can look unnatural and communicate *"I'm pretending to be in control,"* but I've also seen it work when the speaker was relaxed and focused on someone asking a question.

- A modification of this is to lightly hold your hands or fingers together in front of the torso, from time to time. This appears relaxed and comfortable.

- Avoid having one hand holding the opposite wrist. This is a self-conscious gesture that says, *"I feel awkward"*.

- The "fig leaf" gesture of holding the hands together over the groin area can signal, *"I feel exposed"*, if the speaker is uncomfortable. I've seen it work, however, because the speaker, a political candidate, was relaxed and completely focused on communicating his ideas clearly and concisely. His body looked "parked in neutral" and the figleaf signaled *"at ease."*

- Other weak gestures can include holding both hands behind the back or keeping them in the pockets. When the speaker is self-conscious, these communicate, *"I don't know what to do with my hands so I'm hiding them."*

- On the other had, when Conan O'Brien emceed the Emmys, he was pacing back and forth, with arms going from behind his back into the fig leaf. It was perfect for his comedy routine because he was so comfortable inside his skin. He'd had years in front of live audiences and cameras. What would be distracting for a nervous speaker to do worked fine for Conan O'Brien!

- The most effective gestures are specific. Avoid repetitious and unnecessary gesturing, which is distracting and looks nervous and unprepared.

- Likewise, avoid lifeless, unexpressive arms or having the elbows pinned to the ribcage. Open up your arm pits, which imparts a freedom and expansiveness to your appearance.

- I had a lively conversation in a training with Sales Representatives from Mexicana Airlines about how to list items with the fingers *("First, second, third")*. Our different ideas about which finger to

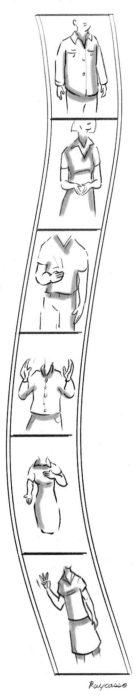

Relaxed gestures put your audience at ease.

start with and the sequence of fingers led to much raucous laughter and fun. Some cultures start counting with the thumb, some with the pinkie and some with the index finger. *"Vive le difference!"*, unless it's going to be distracting to your audience and then, *"When in Rome, do as the Romans do!"*

- When in doubt about using your fingers to emphasize a list of items, begin with the index finger as number one (#1). The sequence is index–middle–ring–pinkie– and the thumb should be the last (#5) finger to raise.

- When numbering, have the back of your hand facing your audience. It's simpler to look at than the palm side, where the rest of the fingers are crouching.

- Finally, hold your hand up intentionally for everyone to see your fingers numbering off the items on your list.

Case Study: Karim Uses Body Language Dramatically

Karim Jaude uses body language to draw his audience into the emotion of his story. He won several Toastmasters' competitions with his harrowing real-life experience of being kidnapped and tortured during the war in his native Lebanon, during the 1970's. Karim describes being interrogated seven times over an 92-hour stretch and uses gestures and movements to bring his story to life and draw us in:"One of the groups slapped, punched, kicked and stomped their feet on my body. Another group tortured me with electric shocks. One of the groups pierced me with sharp instruments—through the nose, the ear, my neck, my shoulder and knees. And yet another group hung me upside down by the feet and whipped me until I bled profusely. I think you get the picture."

**Karim demonstrates the kicks
he had endured.**

Exercise B: Say it with Your Face, Hands and Arms

- Use your eyes, face, arms and hands to express enthusiasm as you exclaim, *"I'm glad to be here!"*

- Do again, be ten times more excited and move out of your comfort zone.

- Make your eyes, face, arms and hands emphasize your main point as you assert, *"I know what I'm talking about!"*

- Do again and be ten times more excited to break out of your box.

- Have your eyes, face, arms and hands express sincerity and concern as you share, *"I care about what I'm saying."*

- Do again, be ten times more excited and leap into the unknown.

- Draw a picture with your arms and hands as you say, *"Sales have increased by 30 percent! By 50%! By 75%! By 100%!"*

- Do again, be ten times more excited and go for it.

- How would you gesture for each of these? "Here, There, I, You, We," Contrast "this with that, No, Yes."

- Do again, be ten times more excited and over the top.

- List these languages of public speaking with your fingers: "Verbal, Visual, Vocal and Visceral."

- Do again, be ten times more excited and over the top

The Legs and Feet

Beginning speakers are often self-conscious about their bodies and uncomfortable about moving. Think about how the legs and feet support us and represent our ability to hold our ground, cover ground and walk the perimeter of our kingdom. How we use our legs and feet reveals the confidence with which we support our ideas and own our passion and power. Eliminate the tell-tale signs of anxiety with these tips:

Weak support and movement speak louder than words.

Exercise C: Say It with Your Legs and Feet

- Practice balancing your weight on both legs and feet.

- The feet should be a few inches apart, with the legs coming straight down from the hips. If the feet are too close together or too far apart, you will be off-balance.

- Avoid crossing the ankles (like a mermaid) or putting your weight on one leg, which causes a hip to jut out.

- Avoid swaying, rocking, doing the box-step and pacing. This body language is not congruent with your purpose.

- Rotate your body weight in a circle, up one foot and down the other. Make the circles smaller and smaller until they're imperceptible. Be aware of your center of gravity. Relax into this balanced position.

Raycasso

Strong support and movement has audience appeal.

Exercise D: Say It with Your Movement

- Practice moving two or more steps towards someone in your audience as you're speaking.

- Practice moving two or more steps as you're transitioning from one idea to a new idea.

- Practice using all the space that you have. Always spend time beforehand in the space you're going to be speaking in. Get used to moving and speaking in it. When I was an actress and toured in "Butterflies are Free", we played a different city and theater nearly every night. The theaters varied in size from intimate little playhouses to very large auditoriums. I always tested out the stage and acoustics before the performance, to ensure that I was prepared.

Exercise E: Say It with Your Whole Body

- Stand and express enthusiasm with your body language. Begin with your legs and feet as you exclaim, *"I'm glad to be here!"* Obviously, you're not going to be standing on one hip and shifting your weight. How do your legs and feet express enthusiasm?

- Now express enthusiasm and add the eyes, face, arms and hands.

- Do again and be ten times louder and more excited. Work your way up to jumping and throwing your arms into the air, as if you're a cheerleader.

- Walk two or more steps towards someone as your sharing, *"I care about what I'm saying."*

- Do again and add the eyes, face, arms and hands.

- Do again and be ten times louder and more sincere.

- Balance your weight and stand tall as you assert, *"I know what I'm talking about!"*

- Do again and add the eyes, face, arms and hands.

- Do again and be ten times louder and more confident.

- Now just be yourself and do the three statements, AS IF you really mean them.

- Again, recording yourself on video/DVD allows you to see yourself the way others see you and reveals the incongruent, distracting behaviors to weed out.

Now, let's move from body language to voice.

Using Your Voice Congruently

Our goal is to project a voice that matches a 100% commitment and conviction 100% of the time. Unfortunately we don't often hear this. When I ask students to name the greatest vocal pitfall, most say "monotone." Flat, expressionless voices accompany many business and technical presentations. Learn to make the most of your voice by following these guidelines:

- Project your voice to be easily heard. Usually, your voice sounds louder to you than it does to others, because you're hearing it from inside your skull, which amplifies it. So when you project louder, you're not as loud as you think. Project your voice out over your audiences' heads and bounce it against the back wall. This signals leadership and confidence.

- Speak slowly and clearly to be effortlessly understood. Many new speakers tend to speak too fast, wanting to "get it over with as fast as possible!" This communicates anxiety. As soon as they slow down and project, they come across with much more credibility.

- Speak in short statements with pauses. The pauses let your audience digest what you just said and give you a moment to assess their responses. The overall effect is confidence and clarity.

- Open your mouth and use your lips to shape your words when you speak. You'll sound clearer and look more open and expressive.

- Practice recording your presentations to hear if you're projecting loudly enough and speaking slowly and clearly enough.

Case Study:
Antoinette Tells About an Unusual Voice

Antoinette Byron, presentation and voice coach and stage and film actress, shares this story told by her grandmother.

The angel turned into a demon when she spoke.

"The importance of an open, rich, expressive voice became clear to me at the tender age of ten. My grandmother told me a story of a train ride she had taken. Sitting opposite her was this beautiful woman dressed in white. As the sun filtered in through the train window, the woman was backlit and looked like an angel. My grandmother gazed at her admiringly. When the train finally pulled into the station, the woman turned to my grandmother and snapped, "What have you been staring at, you old crow?", in a harsh, angry tone. In an instant, the angelic image was shattered. As an adult, I can see that we can have a great presentation, but if our voice doesn't measure up, then our message is instantly diminished. It's crucial to have an open, rich, expressive voice if we want our message to be openly received!

Make sure your voice adds to your presentation!

Use Intonation to Reinforce your Purpose

Now I want to describe how your voice can highlight your meaning and bring vocal interest to your speaking. Let's focus on intonation and emphasis—what they are and how to apply them.

Intonation refers to your musical phrasing. Just as music communicates to us, the vocal music we use communicates to our audience and can either reinforce our purpose or not. There are two primary intonation patterns— downward and upward. When you're ending a statement, if you drop your pitch, you're using "downward intonation." This is called "speaking in statements" and the music seems to say, "It is so!" If you raise your pitch at the end, you're using "upward intonation" and asking a question, "Is it so?" Too much upward intonation leads to "up talk", a musical pattern better suited for television sit-coms than for professional leadership roles because it lacks assertiveness and confidence.

Exercise F: Practice Intonation

Step 1: State "It is so!" and drop your pitch with each word

- Now do this several times and notice how confident you sound.

- Use the downward intonation when you're making assertions and commands:
  "Yes I can," "This is a fact", "I've done the research", "Tell me more"

- Practice making greetings and use the downward intonation: *"Hello!",
  "Good morning!", "Good afternoon!", "Good evening!"*

- Practice the greetings again and be ten times more excited.

- This time, use a downward intonation with dramatic pauses to <u>conclude conclusively</u>, and say *"I… am…finished!"*

Step 2: Ask "Is it so?" and raise your pitch with each word.

- Do this several times and notice that you're waiting for a response.

- Use upward intonation when you're asking a question:
  "What's your name?", "Are you staying?", "How will I recognize her?"

Step 3: Also use the upward intonation to link an idea to the next idea.

- Say your name. Raise the pitch of the first name and drop the pitch of your last name.

"I'm First name (up) *Last name"* (down), or *"First name* (up) *Middle name* (up) *Last name* (down), " *"Martin Luther King."*

- Now link the items on a list, by raising the pitch on each of the first few items and dropping the pitch on the last item. *"Verbal* (up), *visual* (up), *vocal* (up) *and visceral"* (down).

- By utilizing these intonation patterns, you'll be reinforcing your intention and helping your audience remember your points.

Use Emphasis to Make Key Points Stand Out

When you emphasize a key idea, you make it stand out and sound more important than the surrounding ideas. You do this by changing the pitch, volume and tempo of key syllables within those ideas. Go through the exercises below several times, gradually stretching your usual vocal range. Record yourself, if possible, and play back after each exercise. Keep in mind that the more voice you're projecting, the more breath you'll need to take in and release. Also remember that when you're practicing these vocal techniques, you're out of your comfort zone and are not going to sound or feel natural. With practice, this state will subside.

Exercise G: Practice Emphasis

Step 1: Make the pitch higher or lower

- Ask the question, *"Why did we stop here?"*, raising the pitch of *"Why?"*

- This time, ask the question and raise the pitch of *"here?"*

- What do you notice? *When you change the emphasis, the meaning changes.*

- Do this exercise twice more and widen your range more each time. In other words, raise your high pitches and lower your low pitches. Remember to take in and release more breath.

- Do this exercise again—be ten times more excited and act AS IF you really mean it. Breathe deeply and fully and release your voice!

- When you're speaking lower, then raise your pitch to emphasize an idea. If you're already speaking higher, then lower your pitch to emphasize an idea. The goal is to create bold contrast, which makes your ideas "pop."

Step 2: Make the volume louder or softer

- Take these three statements, going from loud to medium to soft –
  (Loud) *"Go ahead!"*
  (Medium) *"Shout your head off!"*
  Soft) *"But it won't change a thing!"*

- Do this exercise twice more and, as you turn up your volume, also increase your breath, open throat and vocal release.

- Use a "stage whisper" for your soft exclamation. That is, whisper and also use a little bit of vocal fold vibration.

- Do this exercise again; be ten times more excited and act AS IF you really mean it.

- To emphasize an idea, when you're already speaking softer, then raise your volume; but if you're already speaking louder, then soften your volume to emphasize the idea. Again, you want your listeners to hear obvious contrast.

Step 3: Make the tempo slower or faster and use pauses

- To emphasize your point, slow down the key ideas and surround them with pauses.

- State *"It will cost the company... hundreds of thousands... of dollars!"*

- Take the first and last parts fast; pause before and slow down "hundreds of thousands", then pause again before quickly completing the statement. Fast!...Pause...Slooow... Pause...Fast!.

- Do this exercise twice more, exaggerating the contrast between fast and slow and making the pauses more dramatic. <u>*Pauses are units of communication.*</u> *The silence contrasts with the voice and is saying something. Notice how a sense of urgency builds during the pauses.*

- Do it one last time, ten times more excited, AS IF you really mean it.

- Now it's time to apply intonation and emphasis to a brief speech.

Exercise H: Apply Intonation and Emphasis to These Statements:

- *"Good evening!*

- *I'm (First Name) (Last Name).*

- *I'm glad to be here!*

- *I know what I'm talking about.*

- *I care about what I'm saying.*

- *I...am...finished.*

- Do this three times, exaggerating the vocal techniques and being ten times more excited.

- Act AS IF you really mean it.

- Then throw away the techniques and be yourself, on purpose and fully associated.

- What did you notice?

JOKE

Antoinette Byron shares a funny example of how intonation and emphasis can dramatically change your meaning.

Say out loud, "What's in the road ahead?"

Now say, "What's in the road? ... A head?"

We use techniques like rungs on a ladder. They help us reach the top; but to continue ascending, we must kick the ladder out from under us and fly. Before you do that, however, it's time to jump back into your Chapter 8 presentation and apply the techniques of body language, voice, congruence and being fully associated. As you're discovering, most of the "juice" is your own perspiration!

Exercise I: Apply Everything to Your Presentation and Bring It All Home

- Practice your presentation from Chapter 8, one section at a time.

- Apply the body language guidelines from pp. 119-124.

- Apply the vocal guidelines, intonation and emphasis from pp. 125-129.

- Be congruent and fully associated.

- When you are satisfied with each section, do a complete run-through from beginning to end.

- Do again and be ten times more excited.

- Throw all the techniques away and do another run through, being yourself.

- Time yourself and note the time.

Exercise J: Breathe Life into Technical and Numbers Presentations

Many of you are going to be giving presentations dense in technical data, jargon, acronyms and numbers.

- Be clear about the story you're telling that underlies the words.

- Apply gestures to paint a picture, punch a point or express a feeling.

- Speak in short phrases with pauses.

- Use bold intonation and emphasis.

- Pour in the juice!

- Read the following three unrelated paragraphs out loud several times, applying these techniques until you've brought them to life and the story blazes through:

1. *"Such a program, working in tandem with TRI (Toxic Release Inventory) would in effect create a two tiered approach. TRI data would provide a broad, generalized, and admittedly crude benchmark of overall toxic pollution performance, while the narrower 'targeted reduction' program would provide explicit targets, aimed at reducing the greatest currently known risks."* [21]

2. *"This program averages the day to day percentage change in price to give a representative unit change. The amplitude of the change is of interest, not the direction. The prices must be recent to be representative, and at least twenty days are needed to give statistical validity to the process. The resulting number is not beta. Beta is a ratio of stock price standard deviation to the standard deviation of the index."* [22]

3. *"Expected utility theory is a very general approach to option evaluation and selection. It involves identification of action alternatives and possible consequences, identification of the probabilities of these consequences, identification of the valuation placed by the decision maker upon these consequences, computation of the expected values of the consequences, and aggregating or summarizing these values for all consequences of each action."* [23]

Speech Therapy or Voice Coaching? "The Ten Symptoms of Speech Pathology Problems": Interview with Speech Language Pathologist, — Katrina Aquiling-Dahl, MS, CCC-SLP

I haven't yet discussed vocal problems such as nasality or hoarseness. If you think you might have actual tissue damage, you should consult a certified speech therapist.

A former associate, Katrina Aquiling-Dahl, is the Speech Language Pathologist with A+ Speech and Learning, Inc. in Las Vegas. I asked Katrina to describe the symptoms that indicate speech pathology problems. She lists ten:

1. Not enough breath for speaking

2. A vocal tremor

3. Inability to say certain sounds (such as the r-sound)

4. Having to strain to get the voice out

5. Stuttering

6. Lisping

7. Weakness or numbness in the lips or tongue

8. Excessive drooling

9. Vocal tiredness from talking

10. Difficulty swallowing; coughing while eating or drinking

If none of these symptoms are present, in my experience, most vocal issues disappear when clients learn to breathe from their diaphragm, to support their voices with the abdominal and lower back muscles and to open their throats. For this, I recommend working with a voice coach.

Summary

You've married structure to spontaneity, poured juice into the container, and are being yourself, on purpose. You're speaking with passion and power and you're ready to go the extra mile to become an extraordinary speaker in your organization!

Notes:

_____

_____

_____

_____

_____

_____

_____

_____

_____

_____

_____

Part Three

Go the Extra Mile!

Rehearsing the transitions between visuals.

CHAPTER 10

Practice With Visuals

Develop Visuals that Work
Build a Checklist for Success

"A picture's worth a thousand words."

— Chinese Proverb

If you're a business or technical professional, chances are good that you're in an organization where speakers read their presentations from their visuals. This is a common practice and, let's face it, it's easier to hide behind the visuals than to confront the fear of speaking or a lack of preparation.

There are other frequent pitfalls with visuals as well. Often there are too many visuals or they're too complex or too boring. We'll address all these issues, but first I want to emphasize that *you can make the biggest difference and even lessen the impact of these other pitfalls by* <u>*rehearsing with your visuals*</u>.

Case Study: I Encounter Last-Minute Changes

Thank goodness I had rehearsed and was ready for what happened during a workshop I was giving. It was about presentation skills, at the historic Biltmore Hotel in downtown Los Angeles and for members of the Public Housing Authority Directors' Association. This was before everyone used PowerPoint slides and, because I was having my audience do several speaking exercises, I used transparencies and an overhead to show them the exercises.

To prepare myself, I borrowed a client's overhead and conference room to practice in. I had eighteen overheads for a twenty-minute workshop and I practiced my presentation everyday, mastering the sequence and the logistics of changing visuals while saying transitions at the same time. When I reached my saturation point ("If I have to run through this one more time, I may throw up!"), I knew I was ready.

When I arrived at the Biltmore, I learned that I was being recorded and, since they had run out of clip-on microphones, I would have to carry a hand-held one. No problem. Then I took one look at the overhead machine and noticed that there was no surface for me to lay my eighteen transparencies on. Time to improvise. A woman in the front row volunteered to hold them. They were numbered and in order. I would hand her the previous transparency and she would take the new one off the top and hand it to me (and my one free hand!).

Because I had rehearsed so much, I was exhilarated by these last-minute changes, which transferred to my audience. The hustle and bustle of my moving back and forth between the overhead machine and my enthusiastic assistant added to the energy, participation and fun. The workshop was a success because I had rehearsed, rehearsed, rehearsed and was ready for anything!

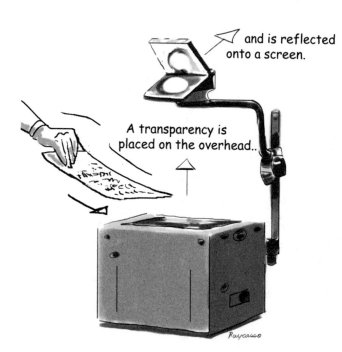

and is reflected onto a screen.

A transparency is placed on the overhead..

The lessons from this experience also apply to PowerPoint presentations.

Excel with Visuals

• Rehearse and be ready for anything

The purpose of all the drilling and run-throughs is to train yourself to achieve the results you want. Become the message; become the purpose; then you will be ready for anything.

• Know your presentation and the sequence of your slides

Because I was prepared, I could handle last minute changes.

When you're the speaker, take charge of your visuals. Know the sequence and content of your visuals so you can draw your audience into the story you're telling. Avoid reading your visuals. Remember, your audience can read. Don't waste their time. Does this mean you should memorize your visuals? No, tell the story behind the visuals. Also avoid talking to your visuals instead of to your audience. How would you feel if your listeners were looking at the person next to them instead of you? Stay connected to your audience. They're why you're there.

• Speak transitions that move you from one slide to the next

What is the thought that moves you from one visual to the next? Speak it out loud. This makes for a much more involving story. Remember the "On a clear day you can see forever!" presentation? As he changed slides, the planner transitioned with *"So that's how clean fuels have impacted our air quality. Now let's look at how car and van pooling have effected pollution."*

• Be the message; be the purpose

Eliminate what isn't consistent with your purpose and your message and you'll be ready for anything! Then practicing with your visuals will put you ahead of most other speakers. But before that, why not create exceptional visuals and steal the show!

Create Visuals that Work

It's easy to fall into the trap of overusing and misusing PowerPoint slides when everyone around you does it. If the company in which you work tends to condone this practice, you can make small changes incrementally.

- ## Use visuals only when necessary

Be selective. You don't have to go as far, however, as Jack Welch, the charismatic former CEO of General Electric, who revolted against visual aids, including PowerPoint software, and banned them from the corporate culture. Welch insisted that the speaker take the spotlight and relate directly to the listeners. I learned about this when I was giving trainings at Honeywell, which was about to be acquired by GE. Welch's policy went into effect and it was "Out with the PowerPoint presentations, the flip charts and the overheads!" Personally, I relished the direct connection between speaker and listener. But then the acquisition fell through, the visuals returned with a vengeance and PowerPoint slides were back to stay.

- ## Simplify difficult concepts with visuals: "Simplify and Stimulate", Interview with Author of "Beyond Bullet Points", Cliff Atkinson [24]

Independent management consultant, author and President of Sociable Media, Cliff Atkinson is the leading authority on how to get the most out of PowerPoint presentations.

Some of Cliff's clients include engineering firms where a standard practice is to use a hundred or more slides for one presentation. The slides and the presentations tend to be complex, difficult to understand and cause what Cliff calls "cognitive overload."

Cliff applies the innovative approach he teaches in his book, "Beyond Bullet Points." He has the engineers simplify their presentations by focusing on what's most important and then by distilling their main message. Next, they develop a story board and use simple graphics with brief headlines to tell their story—one slide telling just one piece of the story. The result is presentations that engage the audience directly, experientially and persuasively.

By following Cliff's advice, you can replace complex slides, difficult concepts and "cognitive overload" with a powerful message and an engaging story that grabs your audience.

Avoid Visuals about History and Features

Many companies take a wrong turn when they fill their canned presentations with information about the history, structure or features of their organization or product. The audience is listening for benefits to them and these slides waste time and are often mind-numbing. What are other guidelines for developing visuals that work and move your presentation forward?

Tips for Professional-Looking Power Point: Interview with Design Firm, Shimokochi-Reeves, and Master Designer, Mamoru Shimokochi

I interviewed Mamoru Shimokochi, of Shimokochi-Reeves, a design firm specializing in the branding and packaging of products such as LA Looks, Silk and Wella. Mamoru is a master designer and he and his partner, Anne Reeves (remember Anne?), have made many sales presentations and project reviews to large conferences and at corporations. Their goal is to grab their audiences' attention with a powerful message and visuals.

Here are Mamoru's guidelines for creating and selecting visuals that work:

- ## Make visuals selective, simple and concise

Visuals should hook your listeners, reinforce what you're saying and be easy to grasp. You want to avoid having too many slides, too many bullets on a slide and too many words in a bullet. Remember your audience can't decode a complicated visual and listen to you speak at the same time. One way to achieve simplicity is to have plenty of empty space to separate your points and make them stand out. For verbal slides, limit yourself to six bullets per slide and about five words per bullet. Keep your bullets spare, simple and short.

Too many words are dizzying. Often when I'm giving a training or working privately with a client, I coach speakers about their visuals. At a training for a financial organization, a speaker showed a slide with the picture of a page from a book. It was filled with words, nothing was bold or highlighted, and the speaker was quoting something. I tried frantically to catch a key word on the slide. Finally, I interrupted and coached him to make the slide over with only the quote—big, bold and brief.

- ## Make your visuals bold and use sharp color contrasts

For slides with text, the font must be large enough to be instantly readable and the color should contrast sharply with the background. If you use pictures, they also must be bold and easy to grasp against the background. For longer presentations divided into segments, Mamoru suggests you change the background color to identify the segments.

• Dramatize with contrasting ideas.

Mamoru also encourages you to apply the concept of contrasts, such as "Before–After", "Right–Wrong", and "Works–Doesn't Work". This is an effective marketing approach that makes your visuals have more impact.

> *A young nurse in my course was enlightening us about heart disease among women. She used a poster of the United States to dramatize her point. On it, she had separated large swatches of red regions in the U.S., where there was a preponderance of female heart disease, from the smaller green regions, where there wasn't. The sharp contrast between the two colors and their implications was shocking and memorable.*

• Create easy-to-understand charts and diagrams.

Pay attention to the thickness of your lines and the spaces between letters. You don't want your letters to look crammed because they'll be difficult to read from farther away.

> *I attended a financial presentation in which my client was participating. Another speaker used a chart covered with four or five finely-drawn lines zig-zagging across the slide. None were bold or highlighted with color. The speaker used a long pointer which added to my confusion. To make an effective chart, the unnecessary lines should be removed and the important lines made bold and identified with color coding.*

• Maintain consistency throughout your slides

Avoid mixing too many type faces or fonts and weed out misspellings. You don't want to broadcast that this is a last-minute rush job. Keep it simple, consistent and correct for a polished, professional appearance.

• TEST!

Stand twenty feet back and see if you can easily grasp your visuals.

Also ask yourself: Is each necessary? Does it hook? Does it reinforce your message and does it move your story forward? If not, throw it out.

Case Study:
A Household Item Becomes an
Unforgettable Point

Mamoru and Anne shared about the dramatic use of a visual as a hook during a financial presentation. To make his point, the speaker used a tape measure first to establish the length of an average 80-year lifespan. Next he asked an audience member's age, which was sixty. The speaker then pointed out how much tape there was between the sixty and the eighty and asserted, "This is how much time you have left; what are you going to do with it?" The speaker's use of an everyday household item made his message bold, brief and indelible.

Exercise: Brainstorm Visuals for Your Presentation

What are your ideas for visuals that would bring one of your presentations to life? Jot them down and then think out loud about how you would integrate each one into your speech.

Next, let's say you've followed Mamoru's guidelines to create and select visuals that work. Then you've rehearsed with your visuals and are definitely in the driver's seat. Now you're ready to set up for your presentation.

Set Up Your Presentation with a Checklist

As the Marketing Director of Shimokochi-Reeves, Anne gives many sales presentations and project reviews. To ensure her success, she uses a checklist. With a checklist, Anne can be confident that she has everything she needs for a purposeful and effective presentation. The following is Anne's checklist:

Before the Presentation:

- Learn background on the client or prospect ("Research, research, research!").
- Schedule a conference room with a projector screen or white wall (for slides).
- Who's going to be in the meeting?
- Can the lights be dimmed?
- How much time do I have?
- Have I rehearsed with everything I'm using for the first time?
- Pack extension cord.
- Computer
- Battery
- Projector
- Cables
- Remote
- Note pad and pen
- Business cards
- Capabilities materials
- Research materials on client and competitors

Arrive Early:

Anne asks for five minutes to set up the PowerPoint presentation so it's ready at the point when it's needed. *Because she has been doing this for a long time, Anne also uses this time to chat and break the ice with the client; however, she advises against novices setting up and chatting at the same time. It would be too easy to get distracted and overlook something!*

- Locate the wall outlets and switches.

- Try not to move anything around without asking first.

- Set up your equipment.

- Focus the projector.

After the Presentation:

- Straighten up before leaving

    After using this checklist for so many years, Anne can practically do it blindfolded and would probably remember everything without the actual list, but doesn't believe in tempting fate. Using the checklist leaves her brain free to bring all her experience, intuition and flexibility to solving her clients' needs.

    Dorothy Breininger adds these items to her checklist:

- Take important phone numbers and get gas for the car.

- Pack brochures and flyers (about her company and products).

- Pack books (that she has authored and sells).

- For a day-long seminar: Take extra water and healthy snacks.

- Ask how many minutes do I have to exercise? Do it.

> ### TIP
> Set up your equipment with audience sight-lines in mind.
>
> Recently I was at a seminar where the audience was seated below the speakers who were on stage. A speaker's open notebook computer was blocking some audience members' view of the screen. Several in the audience became vocal and stopped the presentation until the problem was handled.

Observe Dorothy's 80/20 Rule

Dorothy recommends that you put 80% of your time and effort into the planning—planning your presentation, visuals, rehearsals and your checklist. This makes perfect sense. Think about all the planning that goes into sending a shuttle into space! Your presentation is your shuttle. So ask yourself smart questions about what you'll need to deliver a dynamite presentation; then build your own checklist and use it!

Summary

By taking the additional steps of creating exceptional visuals, of practicing and getting on top of them, and of compiling a thorough checklist, you're way ahead of the pack!

Now here's the last leg up before you jump.

Notes:

_____

_____

_____

_____

_____

_____

_____

_____

_____

_____

_____

_____

CHAPTER 11

Prepare for Questions and Answers

*"It is better to know some of the questions
than to know all of the answers"*
— James Thurber

The idea of preparing for questions strikes some speakers as unnecessary. After all, if they've done all the work to prepare for their presentation, answering questions should be easy. Perhaps, but what will they do with the unexpected question, the tough or hostile question, the speech disguised as a question or the interruption? Will they try and bluff if they don't know the answer? Will they become defensive with a hostile interruption? Will they "windbag" and give another speech in answer to a question? These are some of the pitfalls.

To avoid these pitfalls, go the extra mile and prepare for Questions and Answers.

I coached a newly-elected official after she was caught off-guard when a reporter asked her questions at a ribbon-cutting ceremony. She wasn't prepared and didn't know how to respond. I recommended that, before any and every event, she always ask herself:

- What is the purpose of the event?

- What does the audience want to take away with them?

- Who should I acknowledge for their contributions?

- What are three appropriate ideas to express at this event?

- This would also be an excellent opportunity for a PREP.

And then I coached her to always prepare and practice out loud, even if it's while driving to the event.

Have an Attitude and Approach that Work

Here are some ideas to keep in mind when planning and practicing for Questions and Answers:

• Make Decisions about Q and A

Plan how you want Q and A to happen: In your organization, do listeners interrupt the speaker to ask questions? Or does everyone wait until the end of the presentation to ask questions? Can you ask everyone to hold their questions until the end? If so, and that's your preference, then do so. If, however, the people in your organization are in the habit of asking questions throughout presentations, which is standard in many companies, then be ready for it.

Be well prepared, have an outline and be ready to jot down where you are in your presentation when you're interrupted. Have colleagues interrupt you with questions during rehearsals to ready yourself.

• Be a Powerful Partner

How do you feel about your audience asking you questions? Are you afraid they'll try to punch holes in your presentation, intimidate you or make you look bad in front of your boss? Or are you the new kid on the block, younger than everyone else and nervous that you won't come across with credibility?

In these typical scenarios, the relationship between speaker and audience is adversarial, "You <u>or</u> me!", and invites fight or flight reactions. If you reframe your relationship with your audience as a partnership, "You <u>and</u> me!", you can stay focused on a mutual outcome and respond effectively.

Sometimes audience members really are trying to punch holes in your presentation because the team's commitment is to finding the best solution to a problem. You're part of the team, so stay focused on the big picture, don't take it personally and move forward.

If you're younger and less experienced than everyone else, I recommend you create a support team. Develop a mentoring relationship with at least one of your colleagues, arrange to get coaching before your presentations and feedback afterwards, and be well-prepared for all your presentations. Have your team train you.

• Think of Q & A as Part of Your Presentation

Think of Q and A as still being part of your presentation, even if it's at the end. This will keep you energized and relating your answers back to your message.

• Be Energetic, Vocal and a Force of Nature

If Q and A is after your presentation, walk out from behind the lectern or away from your computer. Move with energy towards the audience and project your voice, *"Who has the first question?"* When someone raises their hand, avoid nodding mutely at them. Instead, walk towards them, gesture and speak, *"Yes, please!"*. After your answer, *"Next question?"* to everyone. Keep it moving with vitality and volume.

If the audience is firing questions at you throughout your presentation, take this same proactive approach. Eye connect, move towards someone, speak out. It will energize both you and your listeners.

• Be Brief

Get to the point and move on. If the audience wants more details, they'll ask for more. Be willing to meet afterwards to arrange a time to discuss it further, if necessary.

• Answer to Everyone

Use your eyes to answer to everyone. Don't lock eyeballs with only the questioner. Pick on different people to ask questions and don't let one person dominate—unless they're your boss. But even if that's the case, answer confidently to everyone.

• Be Prepared to Ask Yourself Questions

Sometimes there won't be an immediate question. Stay confident and answer your own question, such as *"Many times people will ask, 'Isn't it too late to turn global warming around?' My response to that is ...."* Be prepared to answer two of your own questions; but usually one will jump-start your audience. If, however, you answer your own two questions and your audience still has none of their own, then thank them and end the Q and A with a second conclusion—the main message of your presentation and your call to action.

- ## Listen to Questions on Behalf of the Audience

Notice if the questioners speak softly, or with a heavy accent, or mumble, so you can repeat their questions for everyone. From time to time, break up the pattern of repeating questions by paraphrasing them, or by including the words of the question in your answer. Avoid falling into patterns.

- ## After Q and A, <u>Conclude Again</u>!

Usually what happens in most presentations is that time runs out during Q and A and everyone starts leaving. The last idea they've heard was the speaker's answer to the last question. This is not a powerful conclusion to a presentation! So for your presentation, plan to conclude your Q and A with another conclusive conclusion and call to action. *"Remember, a decade ago, we committed ourselves to actions that took a big bite out of pollution. Now, if we're going to turn the tide on global warming, we're challenged to take massive action. We can do it! We must do it!"*

So you would conclude your presentation before opening up for Q and A and then you would <u>conclude again after Q and A</u>. The final conclusion should be stated in a more interesting way and with more juice than the first!

What to Say in Different Circumstances

Now let's address some of the common scenarios. Remember to respond out of partnership, "You AND me!" Plus it always helps to stay away from taking what happens personally.

- ## When You Don't Know the Answer:

No matter how prepared you are you could still be asked something you don't know the answer to. Avoid trying to pull the wool over every ones' eyes. Usually people see through the bluff—and it's more stressful than telling the truth!

The key to telling the truth is to state that you don't know the answer in a confident, upbeat tone. Then you have these choices:

1. You can offer to take the questioner's contact information and get back to them with the answer to their question. *"That's an interesting question, but I'm going to have to get back to you with the answer."* Then arrange a time to do so and keep your word.

2. You can redirect the question to someone else in the audience who knows the answer. But only put someone on the spot if you're certain they can answer. Then ask them to answer <u>briefly.</u> *"That's an interesting question and it deserves an answer. Eric, this is your area of expertise. Would you be willing to answer this question in two minutes or less?"*

3. You could throw the question out to the group, but you have to be able and willing to manage whatever happens. For instance, what if two people have conflicting answers and each insists they're right? I would probably handle this situation with humor and diplomacy—*"You wanted one answer and you got two! Let me see what I can find out and get back to you. Next question?!"* Keep it moving.

• When the Question Is Unrelated to Your Presentation:

Be respectful and let them know that because the question is not directly related to your presentation you would prefer to discuss it with them afterward (there, or on the phone, or by email—whatever works). Thank them and move on. "Next question?"

• When The Question or Interruption Is Hostile:

In this situation, you want to remain powerful and not get hooked by fight or flight reactions of going on the offense or becoming defensive.

1. Reframe ("They're concerned"). Use active listening and paraphrase their message in a neutral, up-beat tone.

2. If there's something positive you can affirm about their message, do so.

3. Answer with the facts to everyone.

4. Then move on with "Next question?"

Case Study:
Speaker Handles Hostile Interruption

Many years ago, I heard a speaker handle a hostile interruption with admirable savoir faire. He was giving a presentation about sexual harassment. This was when sexual harassment was starting to become a hot topic, but before the days of mandatory trainings. The speaker made the comment that

90 percent of the people fired the previous year had been let go because of issues related to sexual harassment.

A gentleman in the audience interrupted and blurted out, "I don't believe you! I know someone who was fired and it had nothing to do with sexual harassment!"

The speaker <u>kept his cool</u> and <u>paraphrased</u>, in a <u>neutral, up-beat tone</u>, "Oh, got it. You know someone who was fired and it had absolutely nothing to do with sexual harassment." He did not react to the man's edgy tone.

"That's right," the man retorted indignantly, "and as far as I'm concerned, that figure is completely out-of-bounds!"

At this point, the <u>speaker concurred</u>, replying, "I know what you mean, when I first heard that statistic, I also thought it was awfully high." And then he <u>answered with the facts to everyone</u>, "But it's in this month's Harvard Business Review..." and he listed three periodicals with this information. His point landed, then he moved to, <u>"Next question?"</u> and everything fell gently into place.

The speaker used active listening to disarm the hostility.

Exercise: Practice Answering Questions

- Stand up and practice requesting that your audience hold their questions until the end. Let them know that you've saved time (be specific about the number of minutes) for Questions and Answers. Maintain an up-beat tone.

- Practice powerfully concluding your presentation and then transitioning into Q and A. Pause in between, allowing your conclusion to "land" before you transition. If you're speaking from behind a lectern or a computer, then walk out during the transition and towards your audience.

- Write down 2-4 non-hostile questions you could be asked about your chapters 7-8 presentation:

_____

_____

_____

_____

_____

- Practice repeating or paraphrasing these questions, or including the words of the question in your answer.

- Then practice answering these questions briefly. Experiment with using the PREP formula to structure your answer.

_____

_____

_____

_____

_____

- Practice again and this time answer to everyone, connecting with one person at a time (use the mirror to practice this).

- Write down 2 hostile questions about your chapters 7-8 presentation.

_____

_____

_____

_____

_____

- Role-play going through the steps of responding to each of these hostile questions (or interruptions):

    1. Release fight or flight tension, emotions, thoughts.

    2. Paraphrase what's been said.

    _____

    _____

    _____

    _____

    _____

    3. Use a neutral, up-beat tone.

    4. Affirm whatever you can about what was said.

    _____

    _____

    _____

    _____

    _____

    5. Answer with the facts.

    _____

    _____

    _____

    _____

    _____

    6. Answer to everyone.

    7. Move into "Next question?"

    8. Practice wrapping up Q and A and concluding conclusively (again), with a call to action.

    _____

    _____

    _____

_____

_____

_____

_____

_____

_____

_____

Summary

When you plan ahead and prepare for Q and A, you demonstrate your leadership at a whole new level and showcase your interactive skills as well. If you think of your presentation as an ice cream sundae, then practicing with your visuals and preparing for Q and A is the whipped cream. The cherry on top is wrapping up your Q and A with another <u>better</u> conclusive conclusion and call to action!

Now you've reached the top of the ladder. It's time to jump again.

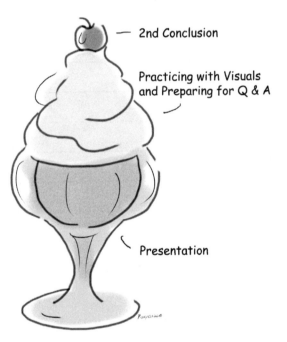

— 2nd Conclusion

Practicing with Visuals and Preparing for Q & A

Presentation

Notes:

_____

_____

_____

_____

_____

_____

_____

_____

_____

_____

_____

_____

_____

_____

_____

_____

_____

CHAPTER 12

Moving from Good to Great!

*"I leaped headlong into the sea, and thereby have
become better acquainted with the soundings, the
quicksands, and the rocks, than if I had stayed upon the
green shores... and took tea and comfortable advice.
I was never afraid of failure; for I would sooner fail than
not be among the greatest."*
— John Keats

Throughout this book, you have been doing what works—preparing yourself inside and out to speak with all the passion and power that's in your soul. You've been learning the drill, from "Take Charge of the Fear" and "Ask the Right Questions" to "Practice with Visuals" and "Prepare for Questions and Answers" and everything in-between. In the beginning, you probably felt, looked and sounded awkward and artificial. But as you worked your way through the book, the steps and techniques became easier, more fluid and natural. You've been learning to "Be yourself, on purpose!"

With consistency, eventually there will be an alchemical moment in your future where "the speaker becomes the speaking." All self-consciousness and "trying to make it happen" disappear. From that moment on, you ARE the mission and the message. This is the magic moment to seek with every presentation you prepare and you can count on it if you're willing to do the work. Perhaps you've already had glimpses of it. The good news is that the more often you go through the steps of preparation, the easier and faster the process becomes—including the emergence of that magic moment!

Passing Through the Four Stages of Mastery

I first heard about these four stages of mastery ages ago and my students continue to find the information helpful:

- Stage One: "Unconscious Incompetence"

In this stage, you're unaware that you're the one causing the ineffective results around you.

Let's say you're reading a report to your high school English class. You're looking down, reading word for word, mumbling to yourself and loathing every minute of it. Only your teacher is listening. There are no questions afterwards and when you sit down, you think about how you hate having to do something so stupid and you and everyone else is an idiot.

- Stage Two: "Conscious Incompetence"

Now, you wake up to the connection between your actions and your results.

Now imagine that you're working towards your MBA or Landscape Design Degree and you have to make an oral presentation and answer to a panel of judges. You know that your results depend on your performance; and you've heard something about eye contact, voice projection and avoiding "uh"; but you aren't sure how to use the information.

- Stage Three: "Conscious Competence"

During this period of time, you're often working hard to get it right—reading books, taking courses, hiring coaches, practicing techniques, joining Toastmasters, studying other speakers. The work doesn't feel, look or sound natural at first, but it gets easier with practice.

This is where you are now, isn't it?

- Stage Four: "Unconscious Competence"

Mastery! Your personality has expanded to include the practices that have, over time, become part of who you are.

This is the goal.

What's Next?

Ask yourself what are the practices that bridge Stage Three and Stage Four? I've mentioned several—reading other books, taking courses, working with a coach, joining Toastmasters. What other possibilities are there? Start from where you are and look at the opportunities in your community, such as professional, political, service and religious organizations, to name a few. Ask around.

Also return to Chapter 4 and review your big purpose. What is your mission in life? This is the guiding principle and context of your actions. Remind yourself often about your purpose.

Here are some of the actions that former clients have taken to catapult themselves into Stage Four.

Case Studies

• *Review Dr. Roy Meals' 2 1/2 year time line and the dedicated actions he took to prepare for his farewell speech. You'll find this on page 72.*

• *Dorothy Breininger took my two-day public speaking workshop at UCLA Extension and hired me to work with her on her seminars and trainings. When she first started out, Dorothy often spoke for free, in order to develop her confidence and ease. Now, she frequently gives trainings and speeches to professional organizations and has expanded her repertoire into a library of keynote speeches. In addition to running her organization and goal-planning services, Dorothy is president of her professional organization and has authored several books, which she sells at seminars and on the QVC shopping channel. She recommends "learning from the masters" and attends events that showcase celebrity speakers from the political, sports, business and motivational fields. Dorothy makes a point of meeting them, forming professional alliances and taking courses they offer to broaden and sharpen her skills. These high profile celebrities include Tony Robbins, Jack Canfield, Deepak Chopra and Dr. Phil.*

• *Karim Jaude, CEO of Dynamics Capital Group, a real estate investment company, came to my "Public Speaking for*

Professionals" course because he wanted to feel more comfortable speaking in English, his third language. At the time, he regularly attended networking events, in which he presented brief "elevator speeches" introducing his business and he also gave work-related presentations. Karim had been a prolific speaker in his native Lebanon and later, in Iran. After working privately with me on his elevator speech and presentations, Karim joined Toastmasters and won several competitions. Now he gives monthly real-estate seminars and keynote speeches; he lectures at a number of academic institutions, including The University of Southern California in Los Angeles; and he has had over a hundred articles published and is working on several books. He ties his experiences of being kidnapped in Beirut and of escaping from Iran during the Revolution to the themes of leadership, motivation and of turning adversity into opportunity.

• While continuing to give sales presentations for Shimokochi – Reeves, Anne Reeves took two 10-week public speaking courses at UCLA Extension, has worked privately with me on her numerous presentations for professional conferences and has participated with Toastmasters International. As a member for more than ten years, Anne has delivered scores of speeches, including humorous speeches, roasts, and evaluations of other speakers. She has served as President of her Club and as Vice President of Education, developing her leadership and mentoring skills. Anne has won several Toastmasters' speech competitions and today, she spearheads workshops designed to help others master presentation skills.

In Chapter One, I described my first meeting with Anne, who was struggling to overcome an intense fear of public speaking. Through the process of preparing and delivering many speeches, Anne climbed the ladder of mastery. Eventually, she reached the upper landing. When her moment came, she jumped off. She describes this leap as she recounts her experience of moving to the top level of a Toastmasters' competition.

"I was standing off-stage waiting for my name to be called, which meant it would be my turn to speak. Suddenly my mind went completely blank and I felt that old fear coming back. Then I remembered my yoga, which I'd been practicing for years. I breathed deeply and released my breath with a long sigh. I knew I was fine; I had stood in this state of readiness many times before and I was confident everything would turn out well, as it had so many times before. My name was called and I walked onto the stage."

Anne won the competition!

Exercise: Create the Bridge to the Next Level

Make a list of actions to take (Is it time to return to Part One's "Taking Charge of your Fear?").

_____

_____

_____

_____

_____

_____

_____

_____

_____

- Choose the action(s) that look the brightest, call the loudest or feel the best.
- Make a plan and begin.

_____

_____

_____

_____

_____

There is no Summary. You and I are at the end of this leg of your journey. Thank you for accompanying me and the individuals I refer to throughout this book. To learn more about some of them, turn the page. *Bon voyage* and remember…

Lean forward and push off with your feet!

Notes:

_____

_____

_____

_____

_____

_____

_____

_____

_____

_____

_____

_____

_____

_____

_____

Who's Who

Michael Almaraz, CCHT
Certified Hypnotherapist
Deeper States Hypnotherapy
www.deeperstates.com

Katrina Aquiling-Dahl,MS, CCC-SLP
Speech Language Pathologist
Speech and Learning, Inc.
www.speakclearer.com

Pat Brady, Editor
!Character Check!
www.centerfororganization.com
818-836-0957
patbrady@yahoo.com

Dorothy Breininger
Co-Author, "Time Efficiency Makeover,"
"The Senior Organizer", and
"Chicken Soup for Busy Moms"
www.centerfororganization.com

Antoinette Byron
Voice and Speech Coach
AB Presentations
www.ABpresentations.com

Donald Dossey, Ph. D.
Author, "Keying: The Power
of Positive Feelings"
Stress Mgmt and Phobia Institute
www.drdossey.com

Pamela Gilbreath Kelly
Pamela Kelly Communications
www.pkelly.com
www.speak-with-passion.com
1-888-593-3951

Ray Harris, Cartoonist
Ray Harris Studio
www.rayharrisstudio.com

Karim Jaude
Business and Real Estate Coach
Dynamics Capital Group
www.dynamicscapital.com

Anne Reeves
Marketing Director
Shimokochi-Reeves
Strategic Visual Branding
www.shimokochi-reeves.com

Kareen Ross
Graphic Design
Book Cover and Interior Design
www.KareenRoss.com
310-397-3408
info@kareenross.com

Mamoru Shimokochi
Master Designer
Shimokochi-Reeves
Strategic Visual Branding
www.shimokochi-reeves.com

Footnotes

1. "Keying: The Power of Positive Feelings", Donald E. Dossey, Ph.D., Outcomes Unlimited Press, Inc., Los Angeles, CA, 1988.

2. A reframing statement could be, "I'm excited about this opportunity and do whatever it takes to support myself." I would then ask myself, "What will support me?" and turn the answers into assertions like these: "I can count on myself to do what works and be prepared. I have note cards if I need them; I drill my opening until I know it backwards and forwards; I greet my audience as they arrive; I picture them in their underwear. I do whatever it takes to support myself with fun, freedom and ease!"

3. "Man and Superman", George Bernard Shaw, 1903.

4. "What's So" Seminar, Erhard Seminar Trainings, Newport Beach Area Center, CA, 1980.

5. "Zen in the Art of Archery", by Eugen Herrigel, Random House, NY. First published in U.S. by Pantheon Books, 1953, NY. Originally published in Germany.

6. "The 7 Habits of Highly Effective People", Stephen Covey, Simon & Schuster, NY, 1989.

7. "Women's Right to Suffrage", Susan B. Anthony, The World's Great Speeches, Edited by Lewis Copeland & Lawrence W. Lamm, Dover Publishers, NY, 1973, pp.321-322.

8. My source for these four distinctions is neurolinguistic programming™, founded by John Grinder and Richard Bandler.

9. "Time Efficiency Makeover", Dorothy Breininger and Debby Bitticks, Health Communications, Inc., Deerpark, FL, 2005.

10. "I Have a Dream", Martin Luther King, The World's Great Speeches, p.753.

11. "On the Faults of the Constitution", Benjamin Franklin, The World's Great Speeches, p. 237.

12. My source for PREP is colleague, Henri Blits, who learned it from a fellow trainer at Hughes Aircraft in Los Angeles. Dorothy Leeds, in "Power Speak" (Prentiss Hall Press, 1988), offers a similar formula, the PEP.

13. "The Mind Map Book: How to Use Radiant Thinking to Maximize your Brain's Untapped Potential", by Tony Buzan and Barry Buzan, Dutton, 1993.

14. The source of this outline is "How to Speak Like a Pro" by Leon Fletcher, Ballantine Books, NY, 1983. This book is an excellent guide for what to say and how to structure your message for different occasions.

15. "Whole Brain Thinking: Working from Both Sides of the Brain to Achieve Peak Job Performance", Jacquelyn Wonder, Pricilla Donovan, Ballantine, NY, 1984.

16. "How Adults Learn", James Robbins Kidd, Association Press, NY, 1974.

17. My source for the three learning styles is Neurolinguistics Programming™, founded by John Grinder and Richard Bandler.

18. My source about being fully associated is Neurolinguistic Programming™, founded by John Grinder and Richard Bandler.

19. "Dunkirk", Winston Churchill, The World's Great Speeches, p. 439.

20. "I Have a Dream", Martin Luther King, The World's Great Speeches, p.754.

21. Land Use & Environment Law Review 2002, Edited by A. Dan Tarlock and David Callies, Thomson West, MN, 2002, p.552.

22. Calculate Risk, A Master Plan for Common Stocks, Robert M. Sharp, Dow-Jones-Irwin, IL, 1986, p.162.

23. Large Scale Systems, Edited by Yacov Y. Haimes, North Holland Publishing Company, NY, 1982, p. 118.

24. "Beyond Bullet Points", by Cliff Atkinson, Microsoft Press, Washington, 2005.

Bibliography

(I've listed by date of publication and put an* after my favorites)

"Beyond Bullet Points," Cliff Atkinson, Microsoft Press, Washington, 2005.*

"Time Efficiency Makeover," Dorothy Breininger and Debby Bitticks, Health Communications, Inc., Deerpark, FL, 2005.*

"Speak like Churchill, Stand like Lincoln," James Humes, Three Rivers Press, NY, 2002.*

"The Lost Art of the Great Speech," Richard Dowis, Amacom, NY, 2000.

"Khrushchev's Shoe," Roy Underhill, Perseus Publishing, Mass., 2000.

"Speak Smart," Thomas K. Mira, Random House, NY, 1997.

"The Articulate Executive", Granville N. Toogood, McGraw-Hill, 1996.

"The Complete Idiot's Guide to Speaking in Public with Confidence," Laurie E. Rozakis, Ph.D, Alpha Books, 1995.

"Presentations Plus,"David Peoples, Wiley & Sons, Atlanta, 1992.*

"The 7 Habits of Highly Effective People," Stephen Covey, Fireside, NY, 1989.*

"Effective Presentation Skills" and "Technical Presentation Skills", Steve Mandel, Crisp Publications, 1988.

"I Can See You Naked," Ron Hoff, Andrews & McMeel, NY, 1988.

"Keying: The Power of Positive Feelings," Dr. Donald Dossey, Outcomes Unlimited Press, Los Angeles, 1988.*

"PowerSpeak," Dorothy Leeds, Berkley Books, NY, 1988.*

"The Self Talk Solution and What to Say When you Talk to Yourself," Dr. Shad Helmstetter, Pocket Books, NY, 1986.*

"How to Speak Like a Pro," Leon Fletcher, Ballantine Books, NY, 1983.*

"Speak and Get Results", Sandy Linver, Summit Books, NY, 1983.*

"The Secret of Charisma: What it is...and how to get it", Doe Lang, Widen Books, 1980.*

"The Quick and Easy Way to Effective Speaking," Dale Carnegie, Pocket Books, NY, 1977.

"The World's Great Speeches," Copeland and Lamm, Dover Press, NY, 1973.*

"Speech Can Change Your Life," Dorothy Sarnoff, Dell Publishing, NY, 1970.*

"How to Develop Self-Confidence and Influence People by Public Speaking," Dale Carnegie, Pocket Books, NY, 1956.*

Index

About the Author

Known for her enthusiasm, accessibility and results, Pamela Gilbreath Kelly has trained business professionals to communicate powerfully since 1986. Her specialties have included public speaking and presentation skills, accent modification, voice and speech and interview techniques. In addition to developing and delivering courses for the University of California, Los Angeles Extension, Pamela has consulted with many academic institutions, corporations and government agencies, in Los Angeles and abroad. Some of her Los Angeles clients include The California Association of Realtors, The City of Los Angeles Bureau of Street Services, Exxon/Mobil, Fluor Corporation, Honeywell, The Huntington, The Los Angeles County Museum of Art, The Metropolitan Transportation Authority, The Municipal Water District of Southern California, Newegg.com, Raytheon and The Southern California Association of Governments. Abroad, her clients have included Yamaha, Hong Kong University of Science and Technology, Singapore Civil Service College and the Singapore Tourism Board. Currently, Pamela is planning book-signing tours, speaking and trainings to further encourage individuals to speak up with passion and with power.

Communicate powerfully;
Powerfully create the future!

Quick Order Form

Phone/Fax Orders: 1-888-593-3951. Have your credit card ready.

E-Mail Orders: Visit website www.pkelly.com

Cash: Check payable to Pamela Kelly Communications

Mail: Pamela Kelly Communications, 1356 Linden Avenue, Long Beach, CA 90813

Please send ___ copies of "Speak with Passion, Speak with Power!" to the following address:

Name _____

Organization _____

Address _____

City _____State_____ Zip_____

Telephone: _____

E-Mail Address:_____

Price: $19.95 US, $31.95 Canada

Sales Tax: Please add 7.75% ($1.45) for products shipped to California addresses.

Shipping US: $4 for first book and $2 for each additional copy.

Shipping International: $9 for the first book and $5 for each additional product (estimate).

( ) Credit Card ( ) Debit Card
( ) Visa ( )Master Card ( ) American Express ( ) Discover

Card Number: _____

Name on Card: _____Expiration Date:_____

Signature: _____

Thank You for your Order!